CRAFTY Little Things to Sew

CRAFTY Little Things to Sew

20 CLEVER SEWING PROJECTS USING
Scraps & Fat Quarters

Caroline Fairbanks-Critchfield

New York

An Imprint of Sterling Publishing Co., Inc.
1166 Avenue of the Americas
New York, NY 10036

ISBN 978-1-4547-1045-5

Distributed in Canada by Sterling Publishing Co., Inc.
c/o Canadian Manda Group, 664 Annette Street
Toronto, Ontario, Canada M6S 2C8
Distributed in the United Kingdom by GMC Distribution Services
Castle Place, 166 High Street, Lewes, East Sussex, England BN7 1XU
Distributed in Australia by NewSouth Books
45 Beach Street, Coogee, NSW 2034, Australia

For information about custom editions, special sales, and premium and corporate purchases, please contact Sterling Special Sales at 800-805-5489 or specialsales@sterlingpublishing.com.

Manufactured in China
2 4 6 8 10 9 7 5 3 1
larkcrafts.com
sterlingpublishing.com

Photography by Chris Bain
Design by Christine Heun

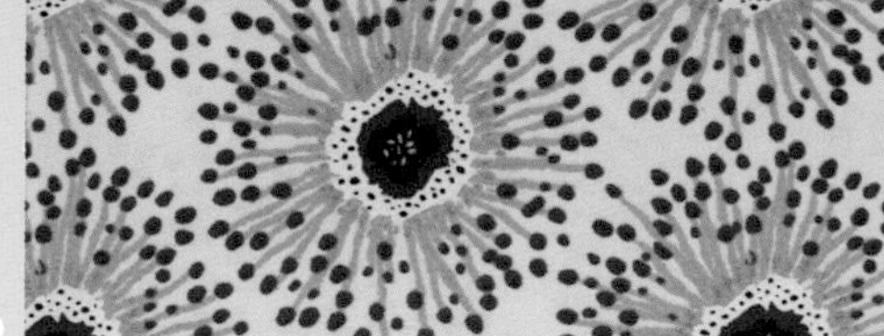

Contents

Dedication and Acknowledgments

I dedicate this book to my husband, who never complains when I sew instead of washing dishes, and to my children, who are my inspiration for everything.

And . . .

Thank you, thank you, thank you to the stitchers, quilters, bloggers, and friends who make up the online sewing community. I love our little world.

I'm also grateful without measure to Wendy, Connie, and the many other creative people at Lark Publishing who showed such great confidence in me, and helped me get this book out there!

And I can't forget to thank the overly generous shops and manufacturers who provided the fabric and supplies needed for the projects and photographs in the book (see Fabric and Notions Sources, page 123).

Happy sewing!

Caroline

Introducing . . . Crafty Little Things to Sew!

Hello, sewing fans! I've been waiting so long to share with you this collection of fun and clever things to sew. The idea for this book came to me years before it was ever published. My sister Beka called me up to say that I needed to write more tutorials for "crafty little things" that could be stitched up in one or two sittings. Finishing a project that you can put to use the same day makes you feel like a superhero!

So that's the idea for these projects—clever items, mostly small, all totally must-have. When I started planning this book, I emailed all my favorite bloggers and was delighted by what they suggested. These are things that you'll want to make right now, and you'll be able to stitch up fast. There are pouches, totes, device accessories, baskets, and more.

SKILL LEVEL

Are you new to sewing? No problem. Near the beginning of each project you will see its suggested skill level with 1–3 "pins." Projects with just "1 pin" are perfect for a beginner or a more confident sewist who is looking for a quick make. A confident beginner could easily tackle the "2 pin" projects. You probably want to have at least two or three other projects under your belt before you tackle one of the "3 pin" projects. Whether you've been sewing for years or you just started last week, you'll find so many pictures, diagrams, and tips that you'll feel like I'm there sewing right along with you.

Be sure to read the Sewing Basics section that's coming up next (page ix). It includes key sewing skills, like basting and topstitching, plus some fun new skills that I know you'll want to try, like putting in a magnetic snap or making your own bias binding.

Let's go sew!

cm
inches

Sewing Basics

Tricks of the trade, stitcher's toolkit, call them what you will; here are some of my favorite crafty sewing techniques. Learn these, and you'll surely find yourself working them into other projects besides the ones in this book.

Basting

A basting stitch is used to temporarily hold fabric layers together more securely than pins.

1 Set your sewing machine for the longest available stitch length.

2 Sew as directed by the pattern instructions, usually just inside the seam line. If the seam allowance is ½"/13mm wide, baste ⅜"/10mm from the edge so the stitches are easy to remove; backstitching is optional. Alternatively, you could simply baste by hand, making long stitches with a needle and thread.

Making Bias Binding

Making your own bias binding is easy, and you can make it cuter than store-bought by using your own fabric. Try stripes!

For ½"/13mm-wide, double-fold bias binding (most often used as an edge finish or for ties), cut the fabric strips 2"/5cm wide.

For 1"/2.5cm-wide, double-fold bias binding (most often used as quilt binding and/or for straps), cut the fabric strips 4"/10cm wide.

1 Cut a strip of fabric 12"/30.5cm or longer by the width of the fabric. Cut away the selvages. Selvages are the edges that run lengthwise along the grain of fabric and keep it from unraveling.

2 Fold one corner down at a 45-degree angle, matching the side edge with the bottom edge.

3 Use a rotary cutter and a long acrylic ruler to trim away the diagonal fold of fabric, and then cut strips to your desired width (A).

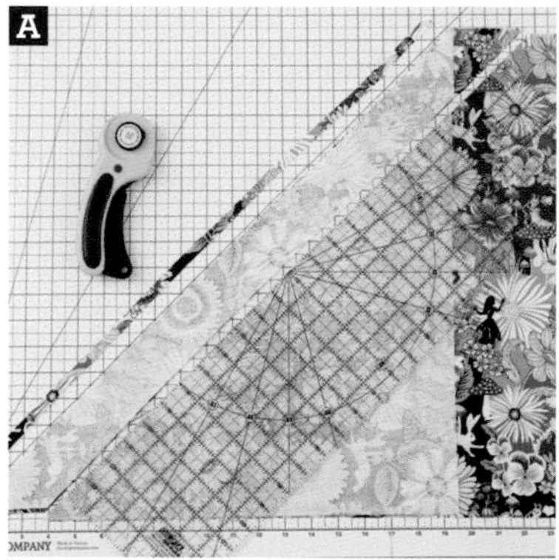

4 Join the binding strips by placing them, right sides together, at a 90-degree angle and sewing from corner to corner with ¼"/6mm seam allowance, as shown (B).

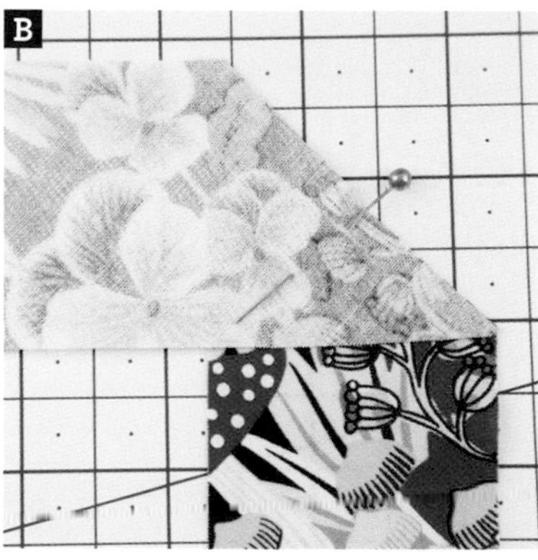

5 Trim away the extra fabric at each corner. Press the seam allowances open.

Pressing Bias and Straight Binding and Other Fabric Strips

I use this method of folding and pressing to make lots of straps and handles, too.

Keep in mind that straight grain binding is made with strips of fabric cut either with or parallel to the grain of the fabric. Bias binding (see above) is more suitable than straight grain binding for binding curved edges, since it is more flexible.

1 Fold the binding strip in half lengthwise, then press (C).

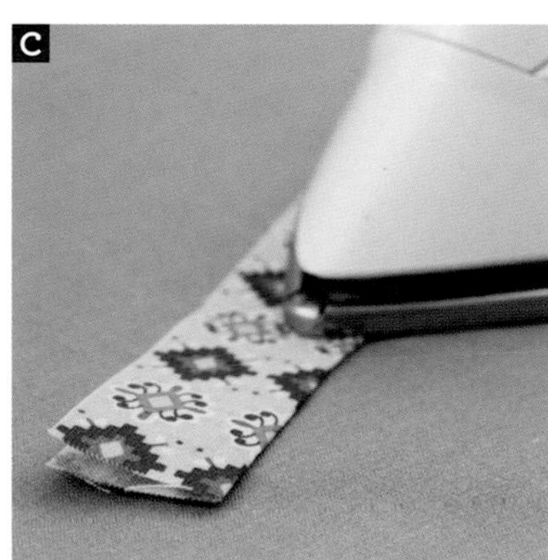

2 Unfold the strip. Then fold both long edges almost to the center fold line and press.

TIP If you press the long edges almost to the center (about ⅛"/3mm from the center), you will be able to stitch the binding in place, creating perfect and uniformly wide binding. Try it!

3 Fold the binding strip in half again, press (D).

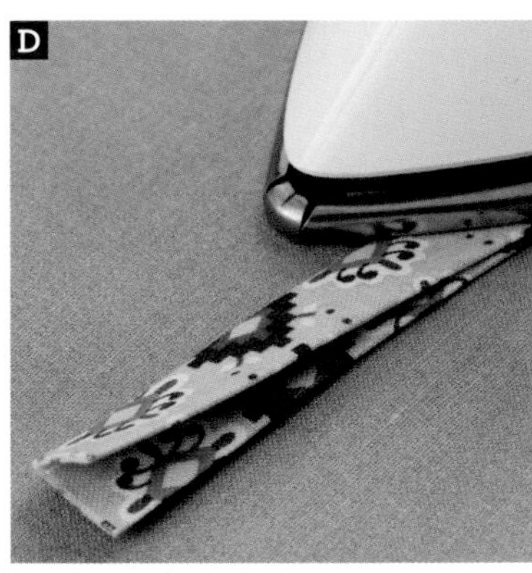

Trimming Corners

Trimming the corners of items before you turn them right side out helps make a neat and sharp corner.

First, diagonally trim away the seam allowance from the corner. Then trim away the extra fabric from the sides of the corner up to the point.

Clipping and Notching

Cutting clips and notches into your curved seams reduces bulk and makes it easier to turn them right side out.

1 For an inward-curving seam, make small clips up to, but not through, the stitching to allow the seam allowance to spread out when the item is turned right side out (E).

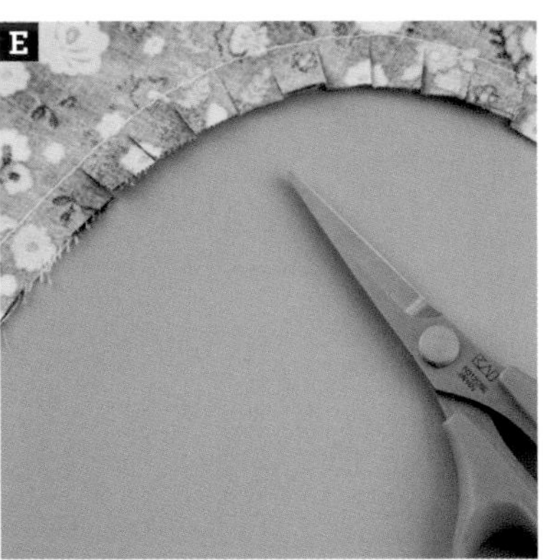

2 For an outward-curving seam, make V-shaped notches up to, but not through, the stitching to reduce bulk in the seam (F).

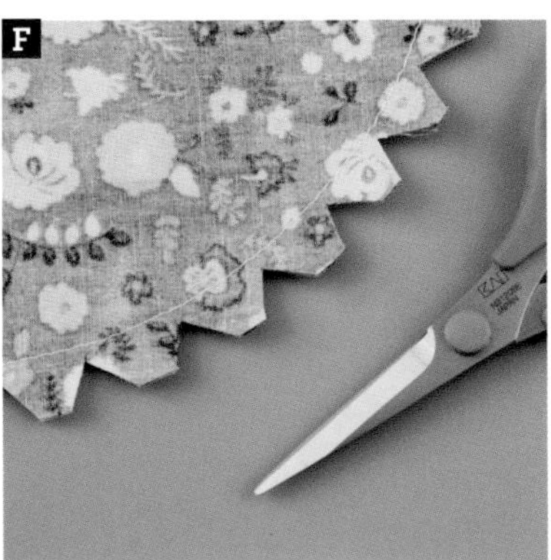

TIP Pinking shears can make quick work of trimming, clipping, and notching all at the same time. Just be careful not to cut the stitching!

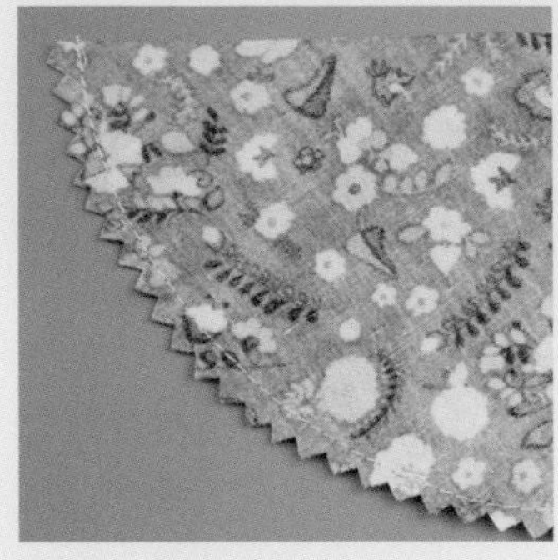

Magnetic Snap

A magnetic snap is a fast and easy closure for lots of different projects. Make sure your fabric at the area where the snap is to be applied is thick enough to keep the snap from tearing through. Adding an extra layer of fusible interfacing in that spot, if needed, is worth the effort.

1 Mark the corresponding snap locations as directed by the pattern instructions.

2 Center the small metal disk over the mark and draw two short lines, using the openings in the disk as guides (G).

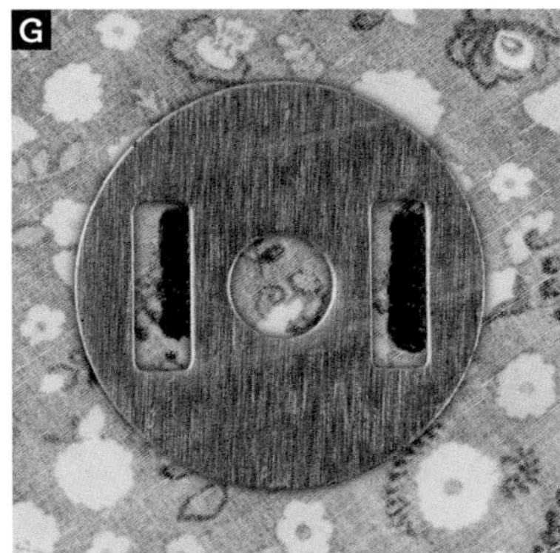

3 Use a seam ripper or a pair of small sharp scissors to cut slits along the marked lines. Insert the metal prongs on a snap piece through the slits from the right to the wrong side of the fabric (H).

H

4 Cut a circle of thick interfacing or felt the size of a quarter and make slits in it corresponding to the slits in the fabric. Place the interfacing circle over the prongs and then the small metal disk over the interfacing.

5 Bend the prongs outward to secure.

6 Repeat steps 1–5 to insert the other side of the snap (I).

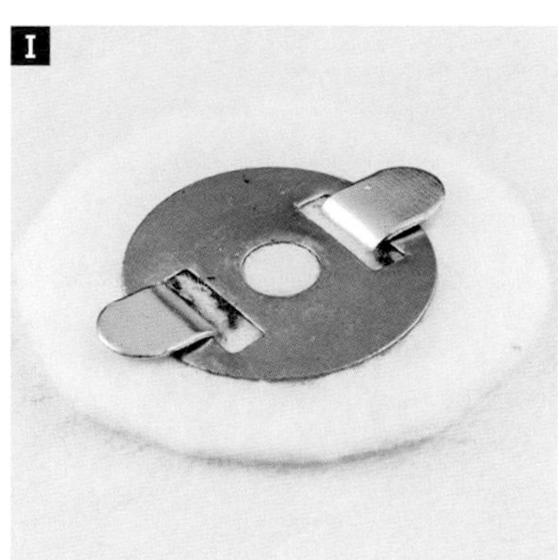
I

Slip Stitching

Use slip stitching (also known as the "ladder stitch") to hand-sew an opening closed when you don't want the stitches to show.

1 Carefully press the seam allowances to the inside.

TIP I like to press my seam allowances before I turn my project right side out. I think it's easier!

2 Use matching thread to sew the folds together by taking a stitch on one side and then the other (J).

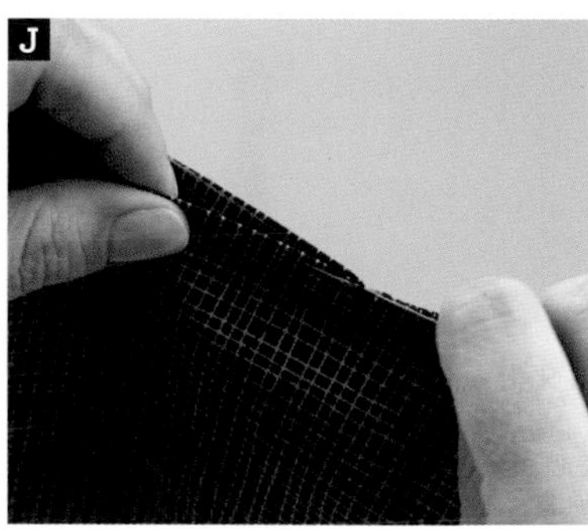
J

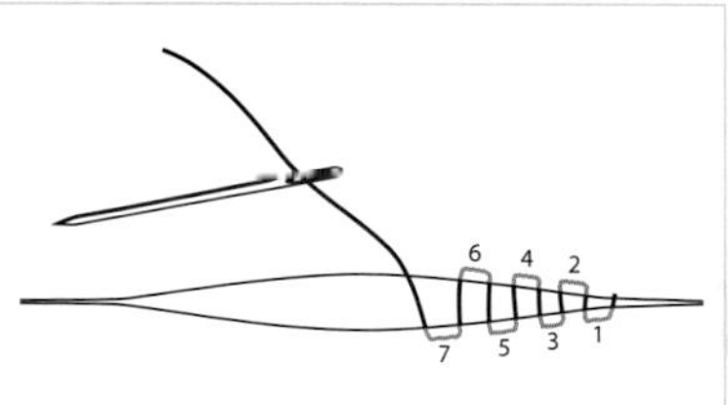

How to Sew a Slip Stitch or Ladder Stitch

Straight Line Quilting

Popular on modern quilts, straight line quilting is lovely on little projects, too!

1 If you have one, install a walking foot on your sewing machine. This foot helps feed the layers more smoothly (K).

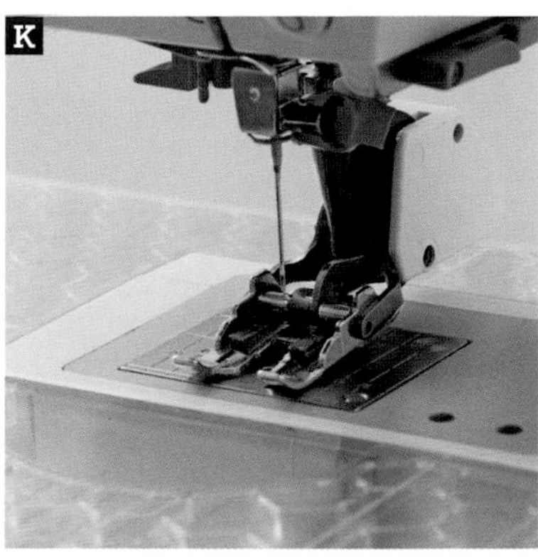
K

2 Pin or spray-baste the fabric and batting layers together with the wrong sides of the fabric against the batting.

3 Use a fabric pen to mark one or more straight lines on your project, if desired. If you find it easier, mark the fabric before pinning or spray-basting the layers together (L).

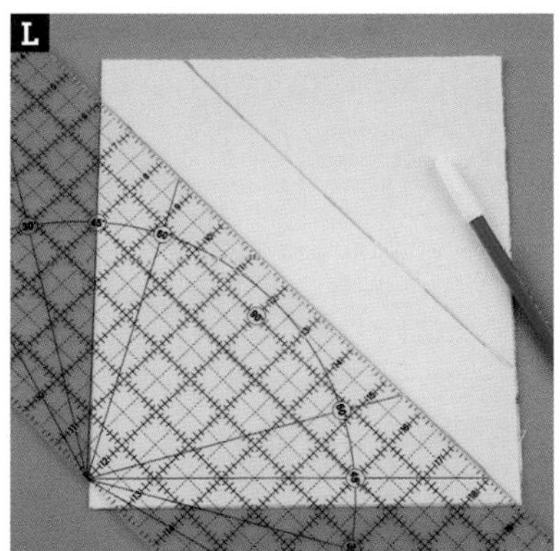
L

4 Sew straight lines of quilting along the marked lines. Add as many lines of quilting as needed (M).

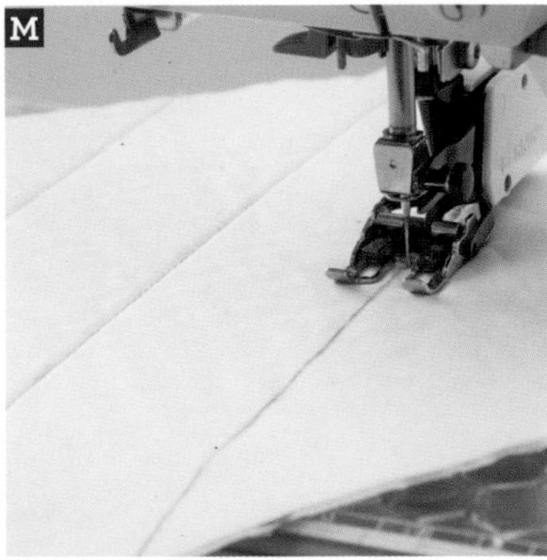

Topstitching

Topstitching adds a professional look to just about any project, as well as strength to the seams.

1 Press the seam allowances toward the side of the seam that will be topstitched, if needed.

2 Increase the stitch length to a medium-long stitch, about ⅛"/3mm long. Stitch ⅛"/3mm away from the seam, on the right side of the project.

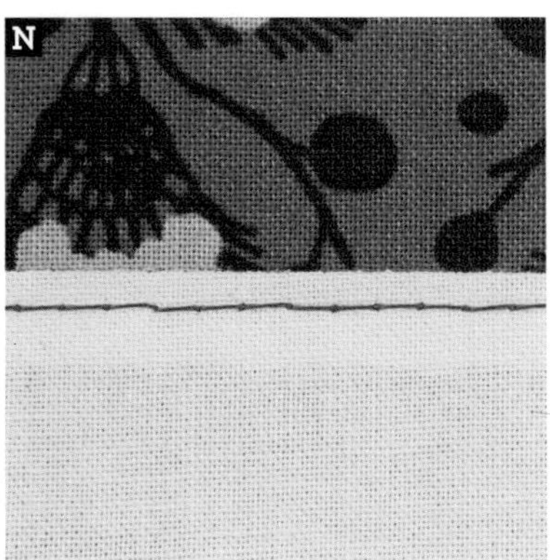

TIP Don't worry and stress if your lines of quilting aren't perfectly spaced. If your work is perfectly perfect who will know it is handmade? I have gradually come to forgive my own little mistakes and love my work because it is handmade by me, not by robots or machines.

A Word about Supplies and Tools

Before getting started, gather together your sewing supplies and tools, including an iron and an ironing board, straight pins and/or sewing clips, hand-sewing needles and needles for your machine, a tape measure or ruler, and cutting tools such as scissors or a cutting mat and rotary cutter. If other tools or supplies are needed, they will be specified in the instructions for your project.

Having everything ready before you begin sewing will make your time spent sewing more enjoyable and fun!

The items in this book can be sewn with either cotton or synthetic thread, according to your preference. When you're deciding on which thread to use, consider whether you want the thread to blend in (a coordinating-color thread) or stand out (a contrasting-color thread).

TIP Topstitching can be done with matching or attractively contrasting thread. Try thicker threads for greater design interest.

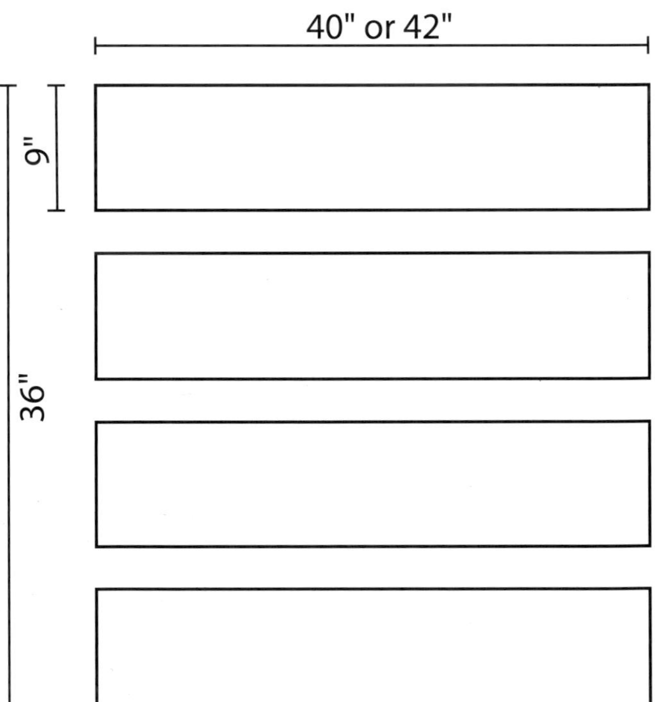

Quarter Yard Pieces

What is a Fat Quarter?

A fat quarter of fabric is special, and not to be confused with the quarter yard of fabric you might receive when you order one at a fabric cutting counter.

A quarter yard of fabric cut the traditional way is 9" (23cm) tall by about 40–42" (101.5–106.5cm) wide. A fat quarter of fabric is 18" tall by about 20–21" (51–53.5cm) wide.

Sometimes a pattern piece that would normally require a ½ yd (45.5cm) of fabric (such as the pattern for the Reversible Barstool Cushion, page 47) can be cut with a single fat quarter instead.

Another reason why I love fat quarters is because so many beautiful fabrics are available in a fat quarter bundles. That means I can get 30 coordinating prints from my favorite designer without having to order 30 yards!

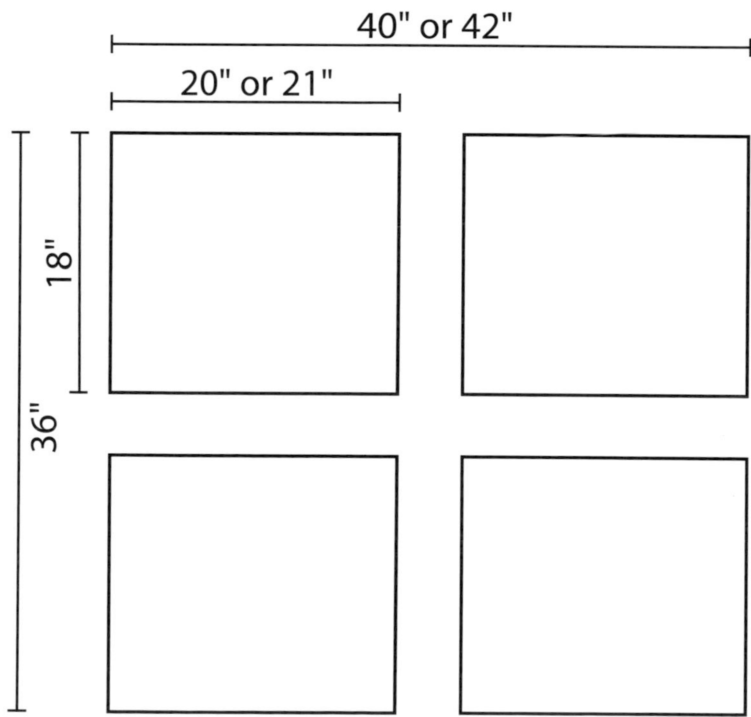

Fat Quarter Pieces

TRAVEL HANDMADE

These days, everyone seems to be constantly on the go—for business, pleasure, and family. Take these handy items along to help organize your life.

Circle Pouch Shopping Tote

Designed by Caroline Fairbanks-Critchfield

LEVEL

This cute tote can hold a bag full of groceries, and it folds into the exterior circle pocket when not in use! It's also reversible, so you can use contrasting fabrics, and switch it up to suit all your shopping moods.

FINISHED SIZE 23" long x 19" wide/ 58.5cm x 48.5cm, including straps
SEAM ALLOWANCE Use ⅜"/10mm seam allowance, unless otherwise noted

What You Need

FABRIC

- 1yd/91cm of lightweight woven fabric for the exterior
- 1yd/91cm of lightweight woven fabric for the lining and pocket
- Templates, page 99

ADDITIONAL SUPPLIES

- Fabric marking pen
- 3"/7.5cm length of grosgrain ribbon
- 1 swivel snap clip that fits the ribbon
- 1 reversible zipper, 8"/20.5cm or longer
- Seam sealant and double-sided sewing adhesive (see Fabric and Notions Sources, page 123)
- Zipper foot

TIP A reversible zipper has a zipper pull that can easily move from the front of the zipper to the back.

What You Do

CUT YOUR FABRIC

From the exterior fabric, cut:
- 2 Bag Body pieces (A on page 99)

From the lining fabric, cut:
- 2 Bag Body pieces (A on page 99)
- 4 Bag Pocket pieces (B on page 99)

SEW THE BAG BODY

1 Transfer the dart markings from the pattern to the wrong side of each body piece (A on page 99) (exterior and lining), using a fabric marking pen. Fold each dart in half and stitch from the edge of the fabric through the dart point on the markings. Fold the darts toward the bottom of the bag (A).

2 With right sides together, pin the exterior pieces around the bag body, making sure the darts match up. Stitch down one side, across the bottom and up the other side. Do not sew the straps at this time. Press the seam open (B).

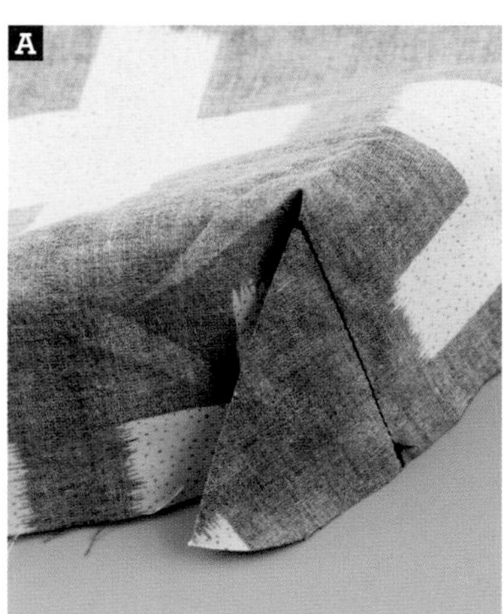

A

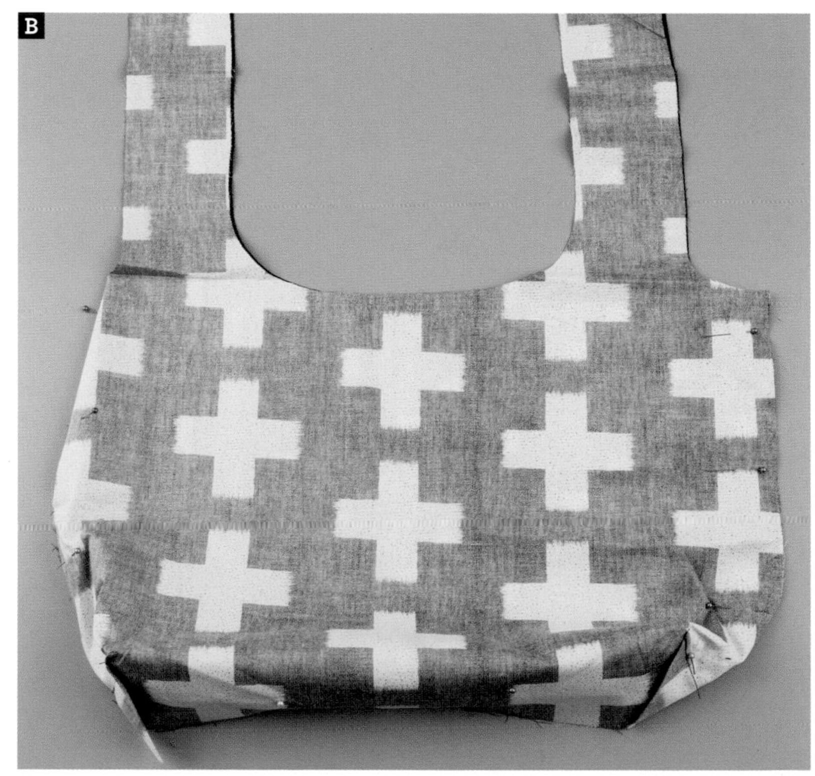

B

3 Repeat step 2 with the lining pieces, except leave a 4"/10cm opening in the bottom for turning.

4 With the exterior bag right side out and the lining wrong side out, insert the exterior bag into the lining. Aligning the side seams and straps, pin together the top edges of the bag, including the straps, but leave the top edges of the straps open (C).

C

5 Sew from the top of one strap around to the top of another strap. Repeat three more times. Do not sew across the tops of the straps.

6 Clip into the seam allowance of the curved seams (see Clipping and Notching, page x). Turn the bag and the straps right side out through the opening in the lining. Press.

FINISH THE STRAPS

1 Press the raw edges of one strap ⅜"/10mm to the inside (D).

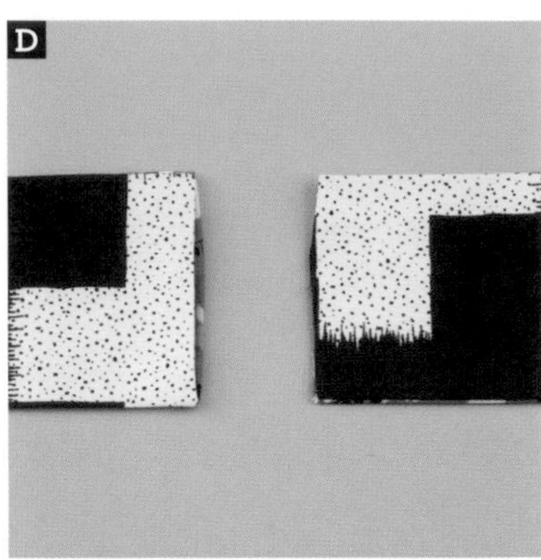
D

2 Insert the other strap on the same side of the bag about ⅜"/10mm into the strap with the raw edges pressed to the inside. Pin.

3 Topstitch ⅛"/3mm from the pressed edge on the strap (see Topstitching, page xii). Stitch again ¼"/6mm away from the previous line of stitching to reinforce the strap (E).

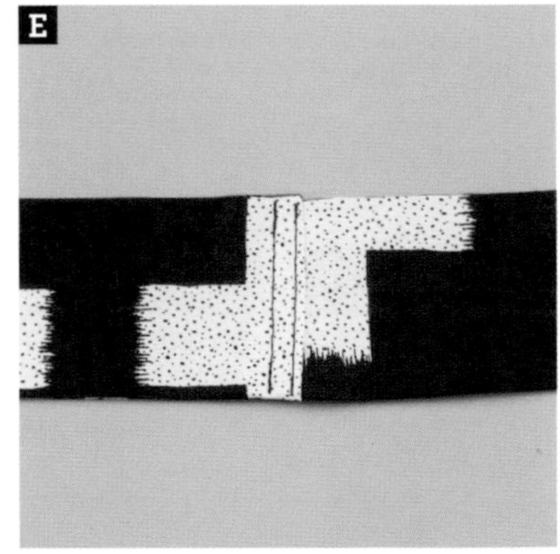
E

4 Repeat steps 1–3 to finish the other strap.

5 Topstitch ⅛"/3mm from the edge around all the straps and the bag opening.

6 Machine-sew or slip stitch the opening in the bag lining closed (see Slip Stitching, page xi).

SEW THE POCKET

1 Fold the 3"/7.5cm piece of ribbon in half around the swivel snap clip and baste it to the side of a pocket piece with the raw edges aligned (see Basting, page ix). See B on page 99 for ribbon placement (F).

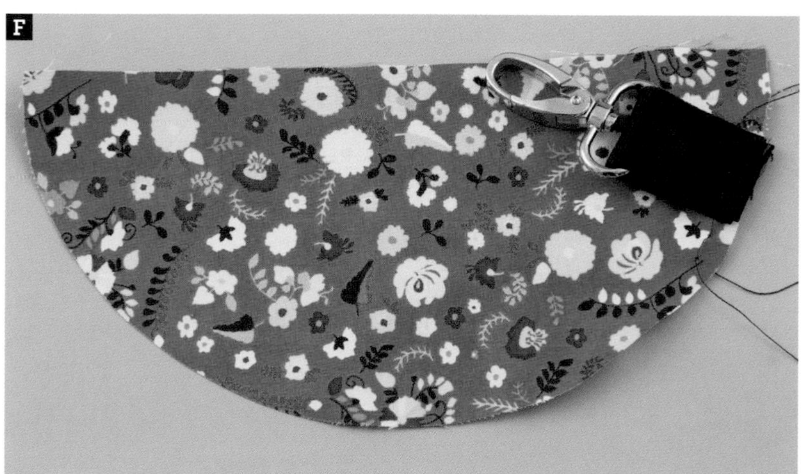

2 Lay another pocket piece on top of the first piece, right sides together, with the ribbon and clip sandwiched between. Pin and stitch around the curved edge. Trim the seam allowance with pinking shears or cut notches around the curve (G).

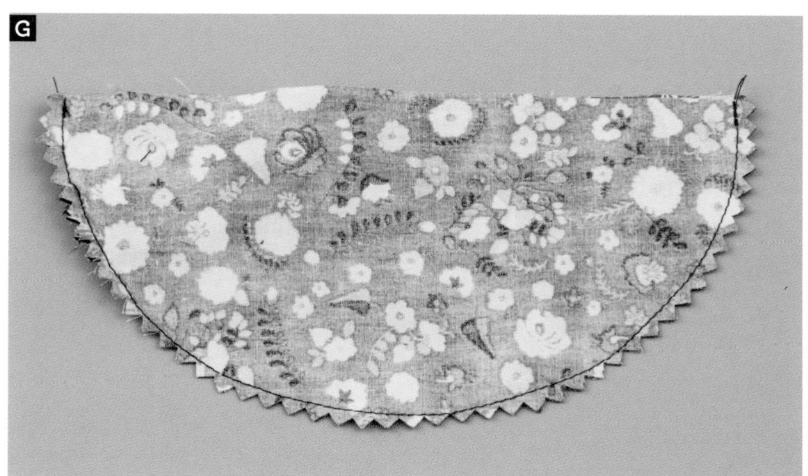

3 Turn the pocket right side out and press. Repeat with the remaining two pocket pieces, eliminating the ribbon tab.

4 Press the straight edges of both pocket pieces ⅜"/10mm to the inside.

INSERT THE ZIPPER

1 Trim the top of the zipper tapes so they extend only ¼"/6mm past the top zipper stops.

2 Lay the zipper over one of the pocket pieces and mark the place where the zipper should be cut to fit precisely inside the pocket. If desired, create a new zipper stop by zigzagging in place over the zipper teeth ¼"/6mm before the cutting mark (you can skip this if you are careful not to open the zipper all the way until after the pocket has been attached to the bag). (H)

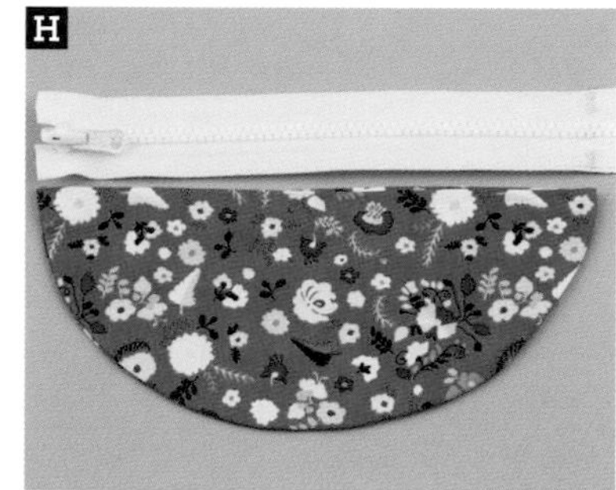

3 Cut away the bottom of the zipper at the mark. Apply seam sealant to all of the cut edges.

4 Apply a strip of double-sided sewing adhesive to each long edge of the zipper tape.

TIP Pinking shears make quick work of trimming and cutting notches on circles—all at the same time!

5 Remove the paper strip from one side of the zipper. Insert the zipper ¼"/6mm inside of a pocket and gently press to adhere. Alternatively, you could use pins to secure the zipper tape ¼"/6mm inside the pocket (I).

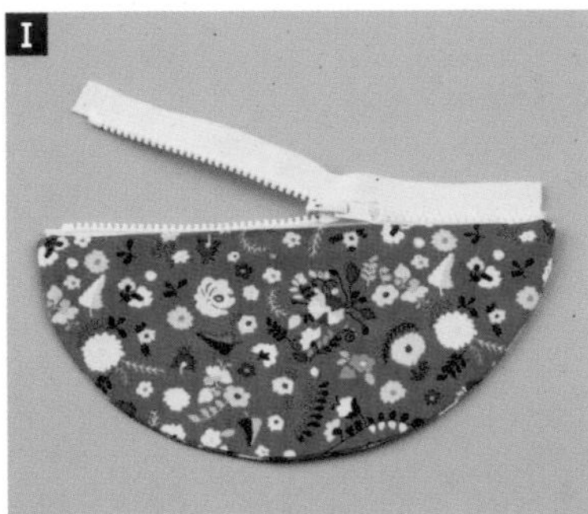

6 Switch to a zipper foot. Topstitch the pocket ⅛"/3mm away from the folded edge (see Topstitching, page xii). Make sure that your stitching catches the pocket on the underside, too (J).

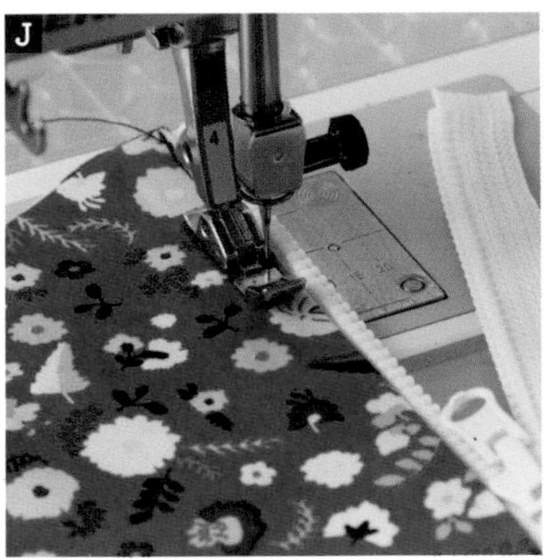

7 Repeat steps 5–6, sewing the opposite zipper tape to the other side of the pocket.

ATTACH THE POCKET POUCH

1 Close the zipper. Pin the ribbon tab to the back of the circle pocket so it is easier to sew the pocket to the bag.

2 Pin the circle pocket to the front of the bag, centered, and 2"/5cm from the top opening (K).

3 Topstitch around one half of the pocket (see Topstitching, page xii), ⅛"/3mm from the edge (between the ends of the zipper). Backstitch and cut the threads. Topstitch around the other half of the circle. Make sure that the other side of the bag doesn't get caught in the stitching (L).

FOLDING UP THE TOTE

To fold your shopping tote into its own circle pouch, lay it facedown with the zipper open. Fold the sides toward the center in thirds. Fold up the bottom and the top, and pile the straps on top. Turn the pocket inside out around the folded tote (M).

Divide-and-Conquer Drawstring Bag

Designed by Beth Wood

SKILL LEVEL
● ●

This small bag is cute and functional. It is just large enough to hold two balls of yarn, a small hand-sewing project, or a pair of dance shoes. There is a handy divider inside the bag to keep things separated. The clear vinyl pocket on the front is perfect for holding small easy-to-lose items.

FINISHED SIZE 6½ tall × 8" wide at the bottom/16.5cm × 20.5cm
SEAM ALLOWANCE Use ¼"/6mm seam allowance, unless otherwise noted

What You Need

FABRIC

- ½yd/45.5cm of cotton fabric
- Template, page 100

ADDITIONAL SUPPLIES

- 1 zipper, 6"/15cm or longer
- Lightweight clear vinyl,* 6" × 3"/15cm × 7.5cm
- Double-sided sewing adhesive
- Zipper foot
- Fabric marking pencil
- 2 pieces of fusible interfacing, 2"/5cm square
- 1 package of double-fold bias tape
- Fabric clips
- Safety pin

* Lightweight vinyl can be purchased in the home decorating department of most fabric stores, but you might also try repurposing other vinyl, such as the bag that your sheets or bedspread came in.

TIP Put a scrap of tissue paper under the vinyl to help it feed smoothly through your sewing machine. Tear away the tissue paper after stitching.

What You Do

CUT YOUR FABRIC

You can use the pattern on page 100 or simply draw an 8½"/21.5cm-diameter circle with a compass.

From the cotton fabric, cut:

- 1 Divide-and-Conquer Bag bottom (pattern on page 100)
- 1 divider, 9" × 12½"/23cm × 32cm
- 2 sides, 8" × 14"/20.5cm × 35.5cm
- 2 straight grain binding strips, 2" × 4"/5cm × 10cm
- 2 straight grain binding strips, 2" × 7"/5cm × 18cm

From the vinyl, cut:

- 1 pocket, 6" × 3"/15cm × 7.5cm

MAKE THE POCKET

1 Position the bottom edge of the zipper, right side up, so it overlaps the top edge of the vinyl by about ¼"/6mm and the tab stops about ½"/13mm from the left side. Use pins or double-sided adhesive to hold the zipper in place. Pins are okay to use here, since the holes in the vinyl won't show. Be careful using pins elsewhere on the vinyl.

2 Install the zipper foot. Stitch close to the bottom edge of the zipper. Trim away any extra zipper to the right (be careful not to open the zipper too much). (A)

3 Prepare the binding strips. First press the short edges of the longer strips ½"/13mm to the wrong side. Then, press all the binding strips, as directed in Pressing Bias and Straight Binding and Other Fabric Strips (page ix).

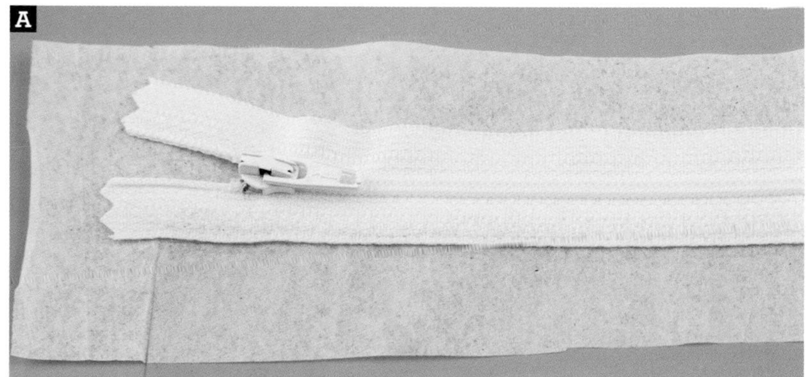

4 Wrap the shorter strips of binding over the sides of the pocket (including the zipper tape) and clip them in place. Stitch close to the inside edges of the binding. Trim away any binding that extends beyond the edges (B).

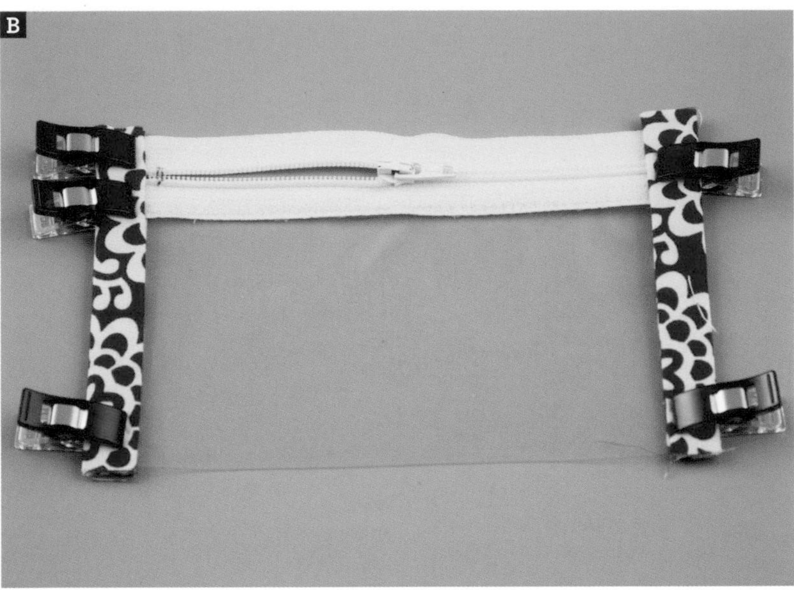

5 Wrap the longer binding strips over the top and bottom of the pocket, so the top binding strip is at least ⅛"/3mm from the zipper teeth and the pressed ends align with the pocket sides. Clip the strips in place (C).

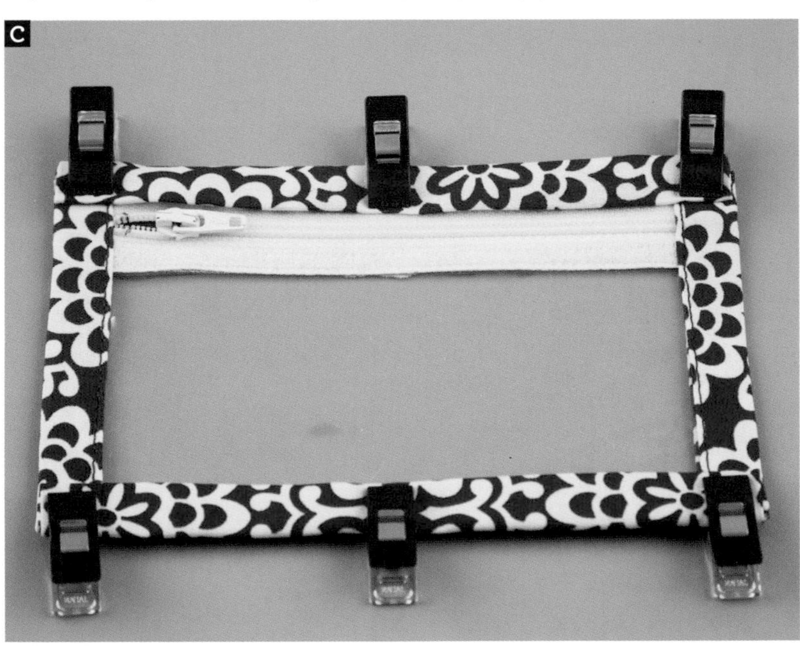

6 Stitch the binding to the top and bottom of the pocket.

ATTACH THE POCKET

1 Center the pocket on the right side of one of the side panels. You can use pins to hold it in place by pinning through the binding. Do not use pins on the visible part of the vinyl (D).

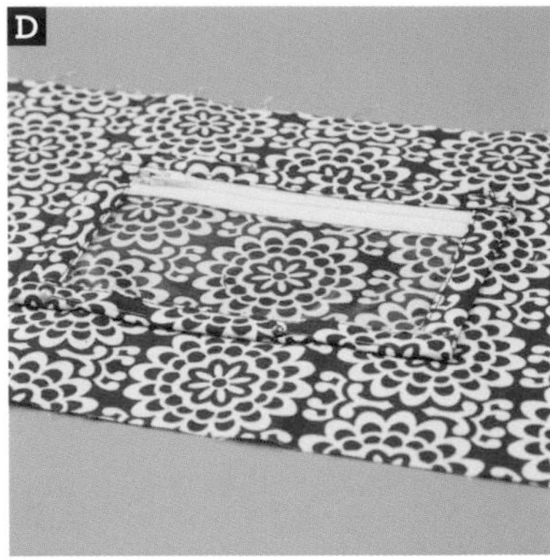

2 Stitch around the pocket, through the binding, to secure it to the bag.

MAKE THE BUTTONHOLES

1 Use the fabric marking pencil to mark a ¾"/2cm-long, horizontal buttonhole on each of the side panels, centered and 1"/2.5cm below the top edge. Fuse the interfacing squares to the wrong side, under the buttonhole markings.

2 Stitch the buttonholes as marked. Cut the buttonholes open (E).

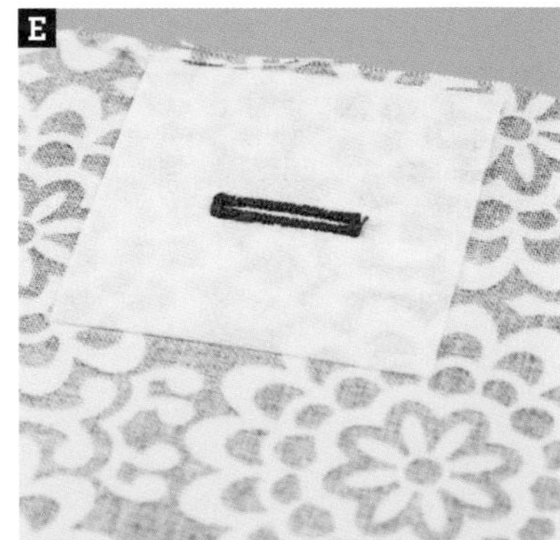

MAKE THE DIVIDER

1 Fold the divider in half with the right sides together. Stitch the shorter edges together (F).

2 Turn the divider right side out. Press. Topstitch ¼"/6mm from the fold (see Topstitching, page xii).

STITCH THE SIDES

1 Pin the side edges of the side panels with right sides together. Then pin the center divider on top, with side edges aligned and bottom seam about ⅜"/10mm above the bottom edge of the side panels. The divider is smaller than the side panels and does not lie flat (G).

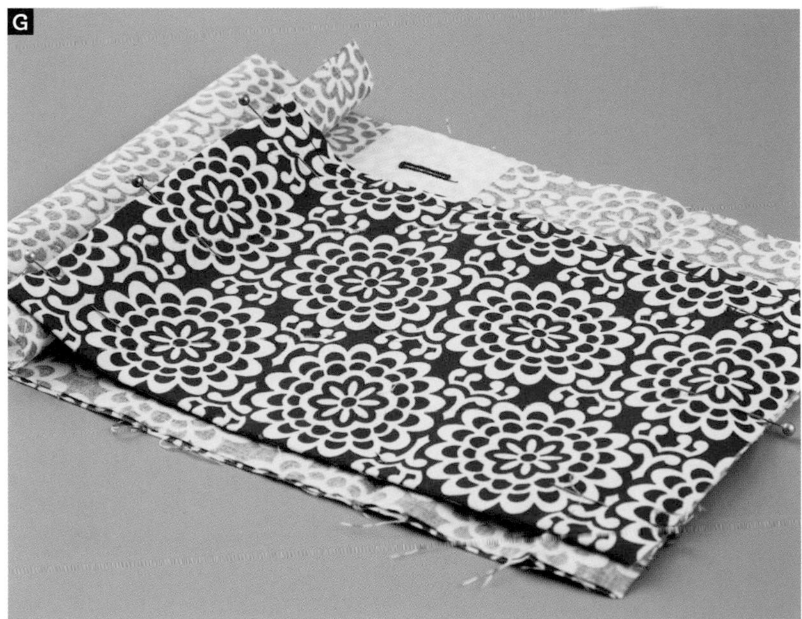

2 Stitch the side seams, including the divider in the stitching. Finish the raw edges with a zigzag stitch or by wrapping bias tape around them and stitching along the edge. The divider is not stitched to the bottom of the bag, but can be hand-stitched to the bottom, if desired.

STITCH THE DRAWSTRING CASING

1 Fold and press the top edge of the bag ¼"/6mm to the wrong side and again ½"/13mm. Make sure the buttonhole is centered under the casing (H).

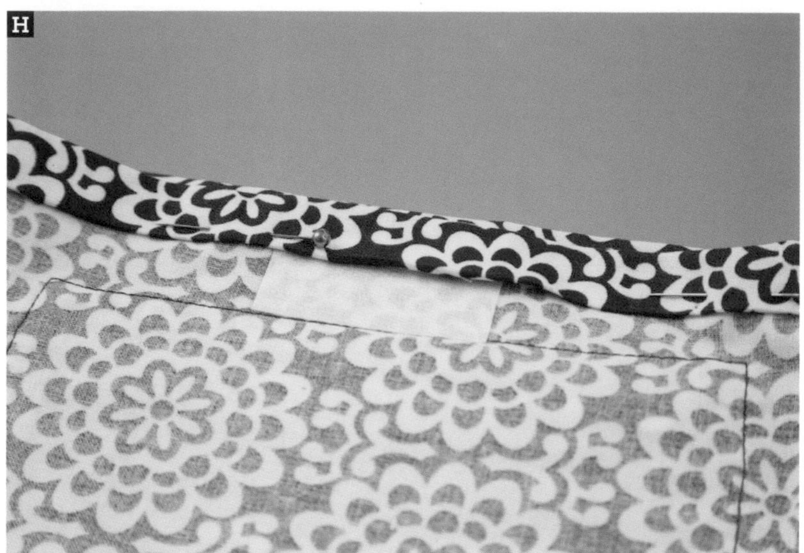
H

2 Stitch the casing in place close to the edge.

STITCH THE BOTTOM

1 Fold the bottom of the bag (cut from piece A) in quarters and press the edges to mark (I).

I

2 Mark the centers of the side panels and the side seams at the bottom of the bag to divide the bag into quarters.

3 With right sides together, pin the bottom to the sides, matching up the quarter marks.

TIP Attaching a circular bottom is easy if you use lots of pins. Since the seam allowance is ¼"/6mm, place the pins in a line ¼"/6mm from the edge.

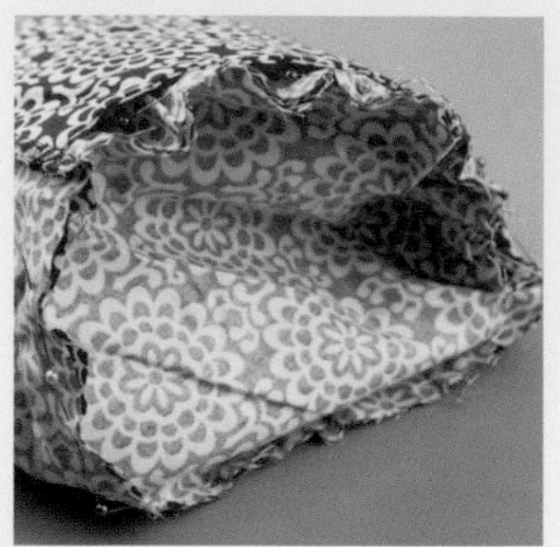

4 Stitch the seam. It's easiest if the sides face up and the bottom faces the sewing machine. Finish the raw edges with a zigzag stitch or with bias trim (J).

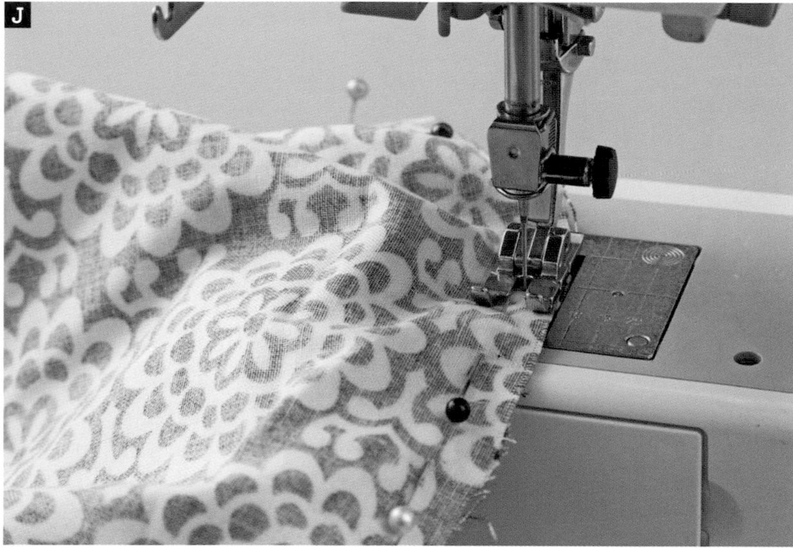
J

TIP If your sewing machine will allow you to move the needle to the left or the right, do so. This way you can position the bias binding over one of the feed dogs and it will be much easier to sew.

MAKE AND INSERT THE DRAWSTRING

1 Cut two pieces of double-fold bias tape, each 38"/96.5cm long. Fold the short edges to the inside and press. Stitch the bias tape closed along the short and long edges.

2 Attach a safety pin to the end of one drawstring and insert it into the front buttonhole. Push it all the way around the bag until the ends meet back at the front buttonhole. Knot the ends together.

3 Repeat with the second drawstring in the back buttonhole (K).

TIP You can also use a cute ¼"/6mm- or ½"/13mm-wide ribbon for the drawstring.

K

Two-in-One Lunch Tote and Place Mat

Designed by Caroline Fairbanks-Critchfield

L LEVEL

This dual-purpose lunch tote features flexible foam stabilizer to keep your lunch hot or cold, and the cleverly designed side flaps unzip to create an 11" × 18"/28cm × 45.5cm place mat on which to eat. Great for kids or grown-ups—depending on the fabric you pick!

FINISHED SIZE (closed) 6" tall × 12" wide × 4" deep/15cm × 30.5cm × 10 cm

SEAM ALLOWANCE Use ¼"/6mm seam allowance, unless otherwise noted

What You Need

FABRIC

Suggested fabrics include light- to medium-weight cotton and cotton blends.

- ½yd/45.5cm (or 2 fat quarters) of main fabric
- ½yd/45.5cm (or 2 fat quarters) of lining fabric
- Templates, pages 101 and 102

ADDITIONAL SUPPLIES

- ½yd/45.5cm of flexible foam stabilizer (see Fabric and Notions Sources, page 123)
- Scraps of medium- to heavyweight fusible interfacing (such as fusible fleece)
- 2 magnetic snaps
- Zipper foot
- 2 zippers, each 10"/25.5cm long
- Fabric marking pen

What You Do

CUT YOUR FABRIC

Pattern pieces are found on pages 101 and 102.

From the exterior fabric, cut:

- 2 side flaps (A on page 101—cut opposing pieces)
- 1 handle (C on page 102)
- 1 exterior body (D on page 102)

From the lining fabric, cut:

- 2 side flaps (A on page 101—cut opposing pieces)
- 1 handle (C on page 102)
- 1 exterior body (D on page 102)

From the foam stabilizer, cut:

- 2 side flaps (A on page 101—cut opposing pieces)
- 1 handle (C on page 102)
- 1 exterior body (D on page 102)

From the interfacing, cut:

- 2 squares, 2" × 2"/5cm × 5cm

PREPARE THE FLAPS

1 Baste (see Basting, page ix) or fuse the flexible foam stabilizer to the wrong side of all of the exterior fabric pieces ⅛"/3mm from the edge. Using a walking foot can make this step easier if you have one (A).

2 Refer to B on page 101 for magnetic snap placement, and mark the tote exterior and lining body pieces as shown. Fuse the square pieces of interfacing to the wrong side of the tote lining piece where the magnetic snaps will be inserted.

A

3 Insert the female sides of the snaps on the tote exterior and the male sides on the tote lining piece (see Magnetic Snap, page x). (B)

TIP There is a mark on D (pattern piece for body) on page 102 that shows where the end of the zipper should veer off the flap. Transfer this mark to each exterior flap piece. As you sew the zipper in place and approach the mark, make sure the edge of your zipper is next to the mark. Sew over both zipper tapes, letting your line of basting end at that mark on the fabric raw edge.

SEW THE SIDE FLAPS

1 Install the zipper foot. Pin a zipper to the side flap, as marked on the pattern, right sides together, and the top zipper stop ½"/13mm from the top edge of the side flap. Let the end of the zipper extend past the edge of the flap at the marking indicated on the pattern. Baste the zipper to the side flap with a scant ¼"/6mm seam allowance (see Basting, page ix). (C)

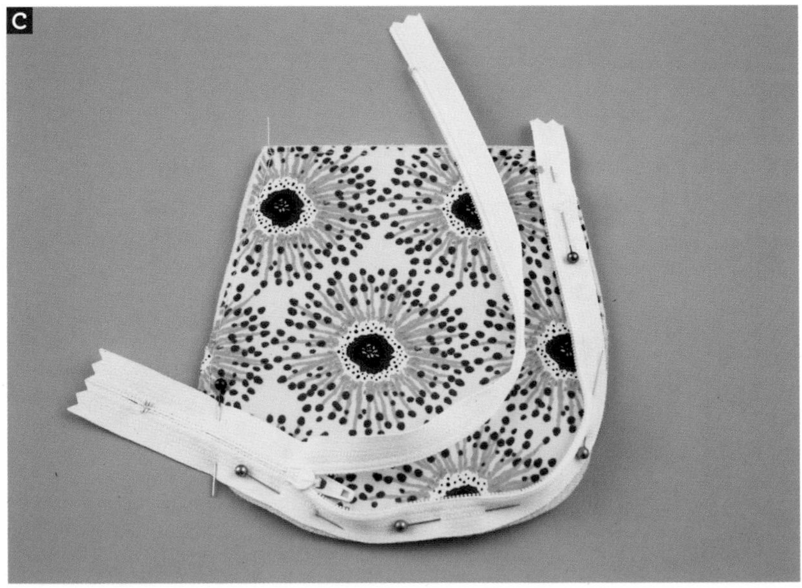

2 Unzip about half the zipper and move the unsewn zipper tape away from the top edge. Pin a flap lining piece on top of the side flap, with the zipper sandwiched in between and right sides together. The end of the zipper (both tapes) will extend from the side of the flap. Only one zipper tape should be visible at the top edge.

3 Stitch along the curved edge, from the top corner, around and over the zipper tapes to the mark where the zipper leaves the flap. You can stick your hand under the lining piece to move the zipper pull, if necessary, and keep the loose zipper tape out of the way. Then stitch across the top straight edge (D).

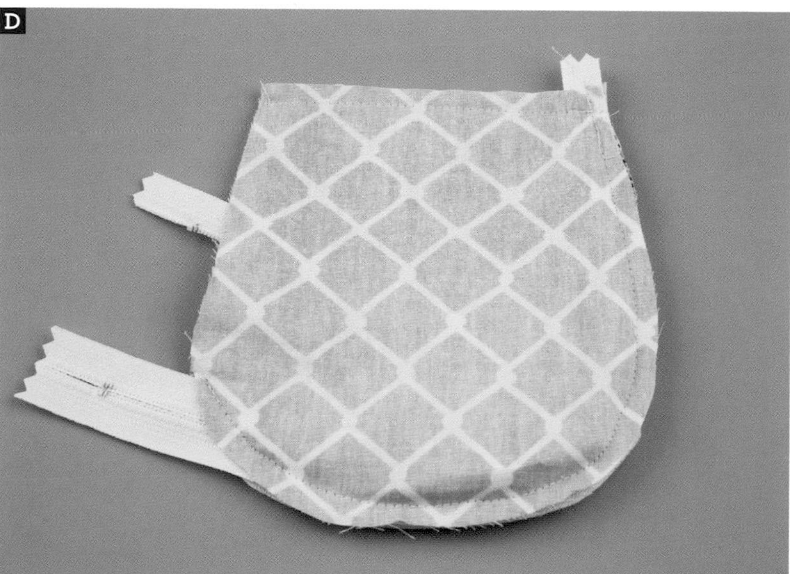

4 Trim the corner and cut notches into the curved seam allowances. Turn the side flap right side out through the unstitched side and gently press. The loose side of the zipper should extend outside the pocket. Cut away the extra zipper tape past the stitching at both ends of the zipper.

5 Topstitch along the seams (see Topstitching, page xii). Baste the opening closed (see Basting, page ix). (E)

6 Repeat steps 1–5 to make the second side flap. Be sure to sew the zipper to the opposite side of the flap so you make mirror images. Set the flaps aside.

SEW THE BODY

1 Open one side flap zipper and pin the unsewn zipper tape to the exterior body on the end with the magnetic snaps, right sides together so the top zipper stop is ½"/13mm from the raw edge. Align the raw edges of the side flap with the edge of the exterior body and pin. Baste the zipper tape and side flap to the exterior, sewing a scant ¼"/6mm from the edge (see Basting, page xii).

2 Pin and baste the remaining side flap to the other side of the exterior in the same manner (F).

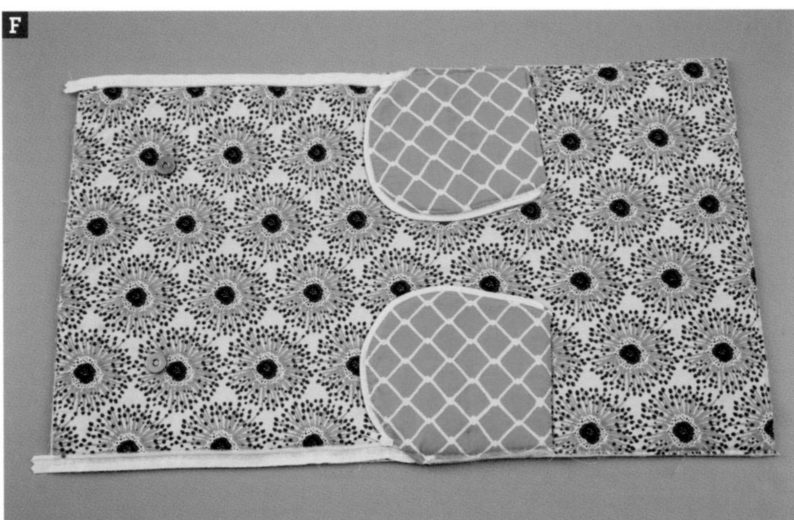

3 Place the body lining piece over the exterior with the flaps sandwiched in between and so the magnetic snap pieces on the exterior and the lining are at opposite ends. Pin all the way around (G).

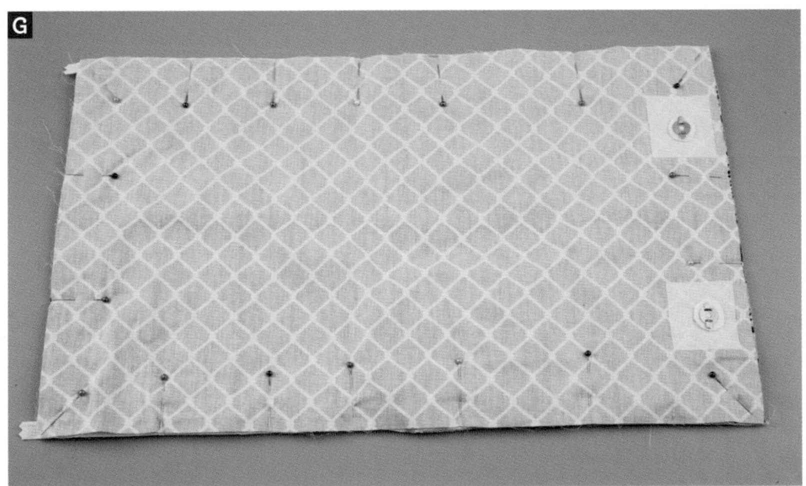

4 Stitch the lining to the exterior, leaving a 4"/10cm opening for turning.

5 Trim the corners and turn the body right side out. Fold the seam allowances of the opening to the inside and gently press. Topstitch ⅛"/3mm from the seams, closing the opening as you go (see Topstitching, page xii).

SEW THE HANDLE

1 Pin the handle lining to the handle exterior, right sides together, and stitch around the edges, leaving a 3"/7.5cm opening for turning.

2 Trim the corners and turn the handle right side out. Fold the seam allowances of the opening to the inside and gently press.

3 Topstitch ⅛"/3mm from all the edges, closing the opening as you go. Set the handle aside.

FINISH

1 Mark straight, parallel quilting lines on the exterior body, the first one just above the side flaps. Then mark parallel lines 2½"/6.5cm away from the first line and each other for a total of six lines (see B on page 101).

2 Quilt the marked lines on the exterior body (see Straight Line Quilting, page xi). Be sure to backstitch neatly at the beginning and end of each line (H).

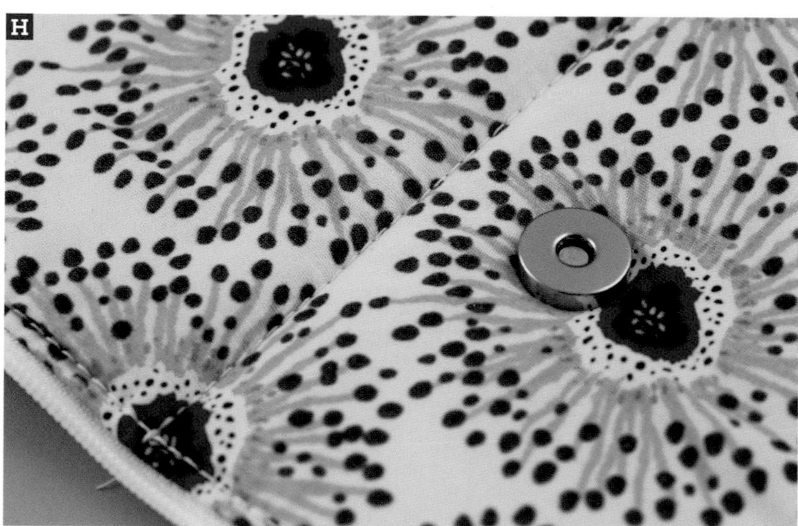

3 Pin the handle to the exterior body ½"/13mm above the side flaps. Stitch 1½"/4cm squares at the ends of the handle to secure it to the exterior body, as shown. Stitch over the existing handle topstitching for three sides of each square (I).

4 Zip up the lunch tote and fill with goodies!

Quilty First Aid Kit

Designed by Tessa Walker

LEVEL ● ●

A handmade first aid kit that holds everything you need to fix all those little cuts and scrapes with love! This one features patchwork on top—and a zipper that is much easier to install than you might expect. The handle on the front makes it easy to grab and go.

FINISHED SIZE 4" × 5½" × 2½"/10cm × 14cm × 6.5cm
SEAM ALLOWANCE Use ¼"/6mm seam allowance, unless otherwise noted

What You Need

FABRIC

We used quilting cotton for all the fabrics that make up this case, but you could use something a little heavier for the exterior, such as linen or sateen.

- ¼yd/23cm of fabric for the exterior
- ¼yd/23cm of fabric for the contrasting sides
- ¼yd/23cm of fabric for the interior (lining)
- Scrap of red fabric for the patchwork cross, at least 4" × 5"/10cm × 12.5cm
- Scrap of light-colored fabric for cross background, at least 3"/7.5cm square

ADDITIONAL SUPPLIES

- ¼yd/23cm of cotton quilt batting
- Quilt basting spray
- Fabric marking pen
- 1 zipper, 14–16"/35.5–40.5cm long
- Zipper foot

What You Do

CUT YOUR FABRIC

For the patchwork cross, cut:

- 4 squares 1½"/4cm from the light-colored fabric scrap
- 2 squares 1½"/4cm from the red fabric scrap
- 1 rectangle 1½" × 3½"/4cm × 9cm from the red fabric scrap

From the exterior fabric, cut:

- 2 side fronts (A on page 103), 1¾" × 3½"/4.5cm × 9cm
- 1 top front (B on page 103), 1¼" × 6"/3cm × 15cm
- 1 back/bottom (C on page 103), 6" × 7¼"/15cm × 18.5cm
- 1 handle, 4" × 5½"/10cm × 14cm

From the lining fabric, cut:

- 1 piece, 7" × 12"/18cm × 30.5cm
- 1 piece, 3½" × 15"/9cm × 38cm
- 2 binding strips, 1½" × 4"/4cm × 10 cm

From the contrasting fabric, cut:

- 1 side, 2½" × 14"/6.5cm × 35.5cm

From the quilt batting, cut:

- 1 piece, 6½" × 11½"/16.5cm × 29cm
- 1 piece, 3" × 14½"/7.5cm × 37cm

MAKE THE PATCHWORK CROSS

1 With right sides facing, sew the white squares to either side of the red squares and press the seams toward the red squares.

2 With right sides facing, sew a white/red/white unit to either long side of the red rectangle and press the seams toward the red rectangle.

(Use diagram on page 103 for reference.)

ASSEMBLE THE KIT EXTERIOR

1 With right sides facing, sew the side pieces (A on page 103) to either side of the patchwork cross, referring to the diagram.

2 With right sides facing, sew the top front piece (B on page 103) to one long edge of the patchwork and the back/bottom piece (C on page 103) to the other long edge. Press all the seams away from the patchwork.

QUILT THE KIT EXTERIOR

1 Use the quilt basting spray to adhere the 6½" × 11½"/16.5cm × 29cm batting rectangle to the wrong side of the 7" × 12"/18cm × 30.5cm interior (lining) rectangle. Then spray the back of the exterior piece with basting spray and adhere it to the top of the batting. Make sure all the layers are centered.

2 Use the fabric marking pen to mark two lines diagonally through the center of the red cross, as shown (A).

TIP Always test fabric marking pens or pencils on scrap fabric first to make sure they will not leave unwanted marks on your fabric.

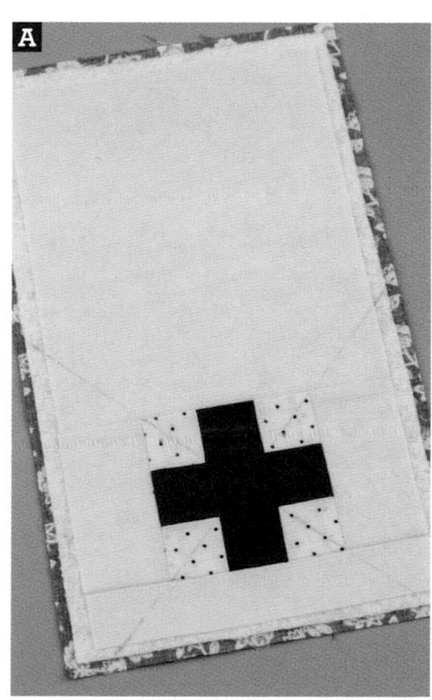

3 Stitch on the marked lines to quilt the three layers together. Continue stitching straight lines ⅝"/16mm apart on each side of the marked lines until the entire piece is quilted (see Straight Line Quilting, page xi). (B)

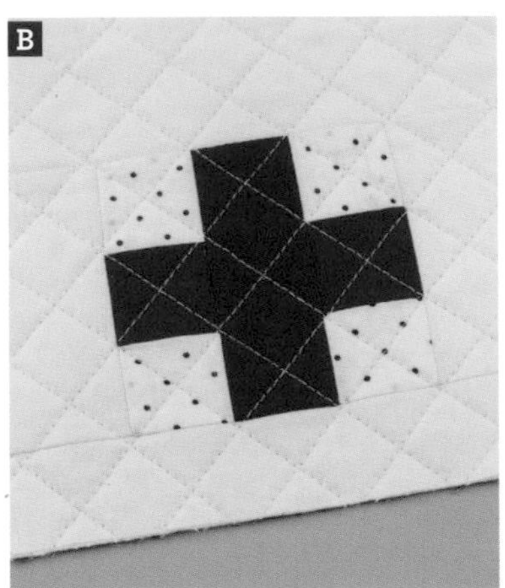
B

4 Trim away the extra batting and interior (lining) fabric and straighten the edges, if necessary. The exterior piece should now measure 6" x 11"/15cm x 28cm.

5 Mark the exterior piece by snipping ¼"/6mm into the seam allowance at the marks indicated on the long edges, as shown on the diagram on page 104.

6 Using something small and round as a template (a spool of thread works great), mark four round corners. Cut along the markings (C).

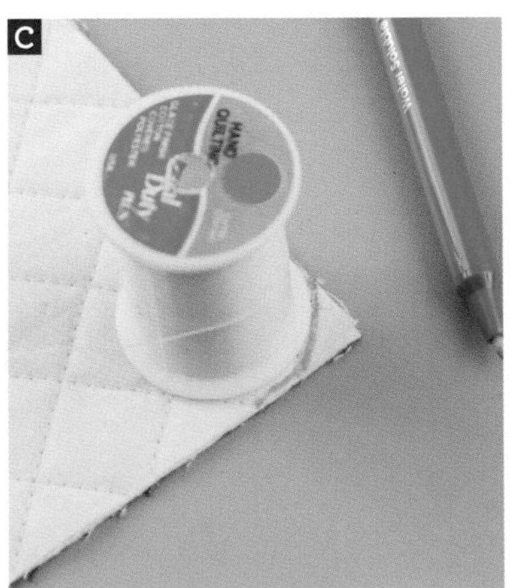
C

MAKE AND QUILT THE SIDE PIECE

1 Use the quilt basting spray to adhere the 3" × 14½"/7.5cm × 37cm batting rectangle to the wrong side of the 3½" × 15"/9cm × 38cm interior lining rectangle. Then spray the back of the 2½" × 14"/6.5cm × 35.5cm contrasting exterior rectangle piece with basting spray and adhere it to the top of the batting. Make sure that all the layers are centered. Starting in the center, mark and stitch a line crosswise through all the layers.

2 Stitch parallel lines ½"/13mm apart on both sides of the first line until the entire piece is quilted. Trim away the extra lining fabric and batting and straighten the edges, if necessary. This piece should measure 14" × 2½"/35.5cm × 6.5cm (D).

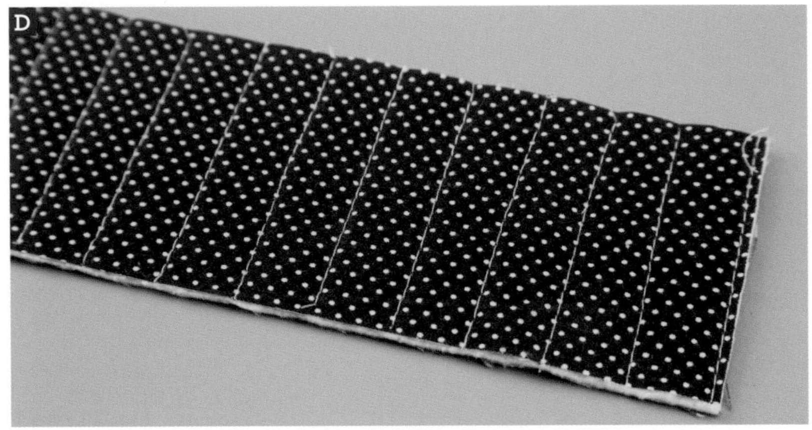
D

MAKE AND ATTACH THE HANDLE

1 Fold and press the handle piece as directed in the Straight Grain Binding section, page ix.

2 Topstitch the handle ⅛"/3mm away from each long edge (see Topstitching, page xii).

3 Fold each short end of the handle ½"/13mm to the back and press well.

4 Make a mark 2"/5cm away from each side of the center of the side piece. Pin the folded edges of the handle along these two marks, allowing for some slack in the handle. Stitch the handle in place by sewing a small rectangle, enclosing the raw edges at each end under the stitching (E).

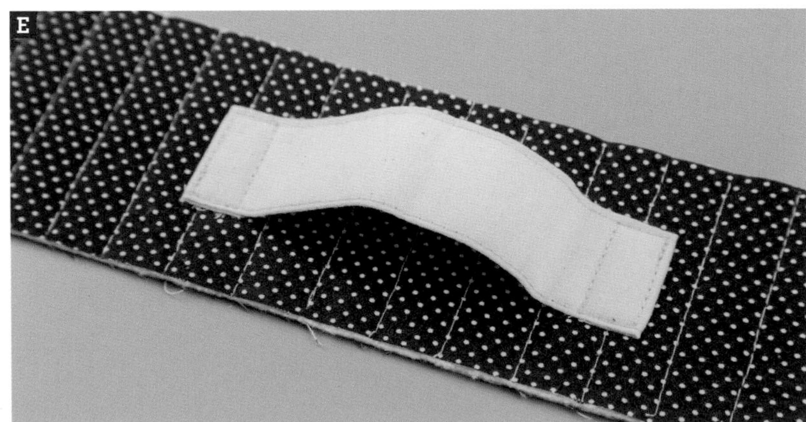
E

ATTACH THE ZIPPER

1 Find the center of the zipper by folding it in half. Mark the center on both sides of the zipper teeth. You might need to gently press the zipper first.

2 Open the zipper and place it facedown on the right side of the exterior piece, matching the center mark on the zipper with the center mark on the short edge of the exterior nearest the patchwork cross. Pin the zipper in place, starting at the center and continuing outward toward both ends. Make small clips in the zipper tape to help ease it around the corners.

TIP Centering the zipper like this ensures that you don't end up with a wonky zipper!

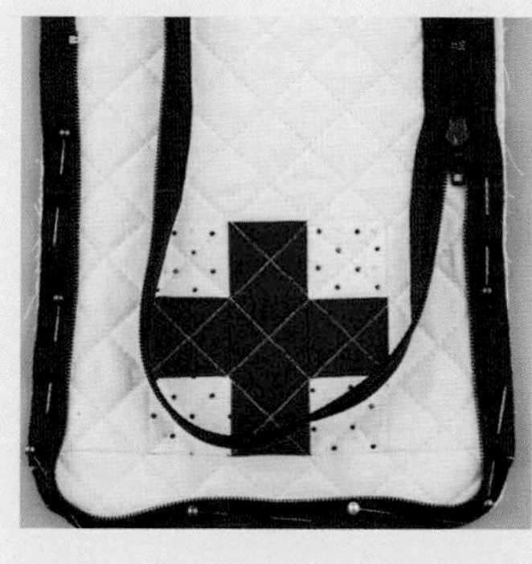

3 Install the zipper foot. Stitch the zipper to the exterior. Start and stop stitching at the marks that you made (and clipped) on the long edges of the exterior piece. Transfer the marks to the zipper tape, if necessary. Don't worry about the excess zipper; it will be trimmed off later. Neaten the raw edges of the seam with a zigzag stitch, if desired.

4 Turn the zipper tape to the inside and press. Topstitch ⅛"/3mm from the seam (see Topstitching, page xii). Take care not to stitch beyond the clipped marks (F).

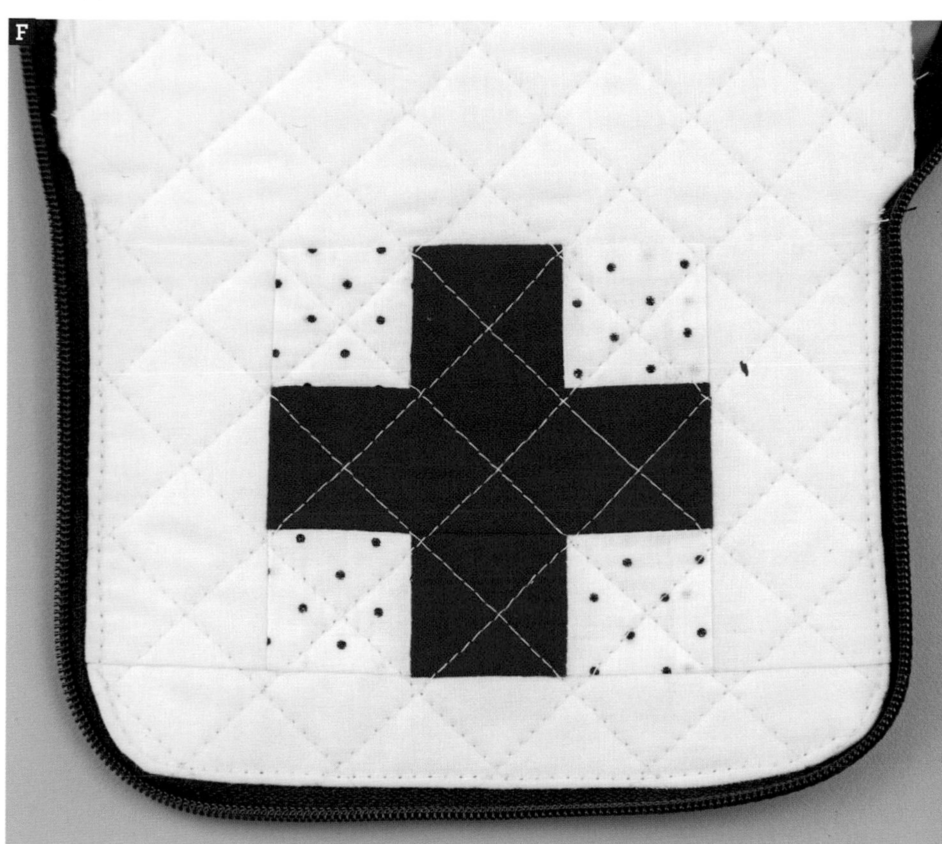

5 On the side piece, mark the center of the long edges in the seam allowance. Then make a mark on each side ¼"/6mm from the end.

6 Place the other side of the zipper tape face down on the side piece, matching the centers. Pin the center and continue pinning to each edge.

7 Stitch the zipper to the side piece, starting and stopping at the marks that are ¼"/6mm from the ends. Neaten the raw edges of the seam with a zigzag stitch.

8 Press the seam allowance to the wrong side and topstitch ⅛"/3mm from the zipper seam.

ASSEMBLE THE KIT

Before starting this step, make sure the zipper is halfway open so that you will be able to turn the piece after stitching the seams.

1 With right sides together, pin the remaining long edge of the side piece to the other side of the exterior. Again, begin in the center and work toward the ends. Match the center mark on the side piece to the center mark on the bottom of the case. Match the marks that are ¼"/6mm from the ends of the side piece to the remaining clips on the exterior. Make several clips within the seam allowance of the side piece where it aligns with the exterior corners so it is easier to stitch the pieces together smoothly (G).

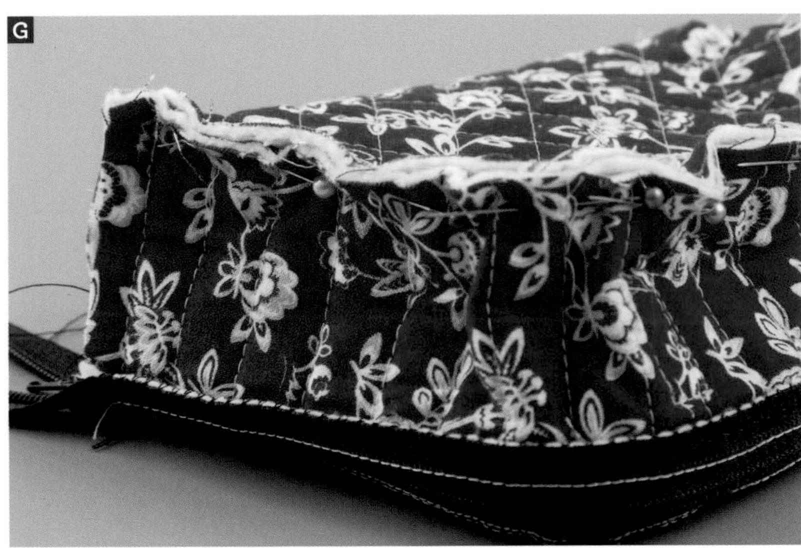

2 Stitch, starting and stopping at the marks that are ¼"/6mm from the ends. Neaten the raw edges of the seam with a zigzag stitch. Press the seam allowance toward the side piece and topstitch ⅛"/3mm from the edge (see Topstitching, page xii).

TIP Copy the marks that are ¼"/6mm from the ends of the side piece onto the zipper tape.

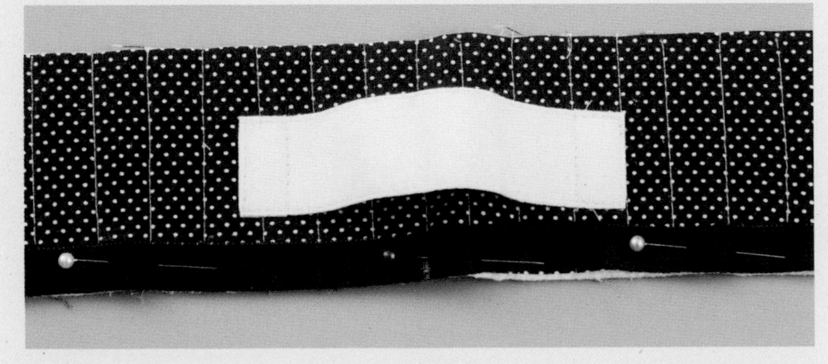

3 To finish, keep the kit wrong side out and match up the raw edge of the quilted side piece with the remaining unstitched section of the exterior (between the clips). The clips into the seam allowance will allow you to spread the fabric at the corners of the exterior piece. The zipper will lie flat against the quilted side piece. Pin (H).

4 Stitch between the clipped marks, including over the zipper teeth. The seam will catch the end of the zipper, which can then be trimmed even with the raw edges of the fabrics. Trim away the extra zipper.

5 Repeat step 4 on the opposite side. You will need to pin both zipper tapes in place and catch them in the stitching (I).

I

ENCASE THE INTERIOR RAW EDGES

1 Fold and press the 1½" × 4"/4cm × 10cm binding strips as directed in Pressing Bias and Straight Binding and Other Fabric Strips (page ix). (J)

2 With right sides together, center a binding strip over the raw edge of one of the interior side seams and stitch. Tuck in the short edges and turn the fabric strip to the other side, encasing the raw edge. Stitch close to the folded edge. Repeat for the opposite side seam (K).

J

K

75¢
SAVE
SAVE
save

Casual Couponer Divided Pouch

Designed by Sarah Markos

L LEVEL ● ●

This little pouch is designed for the thrifty—and stylish—shopper. It's the perfect size to throw in a purse or backpack to carry all those store coupons you're always losing. The three dividers inside make it so easy to use, and the cute ribbon tabs keep things neat and orderly.

FINISHED SIZE Approximately 5¾" x 9½"/14.5cm × 24cm
SEAM ALLOWANCE Use ¼"/6mm seam allowance, unless otherwise noted

What You Need

FABRIC

Suggested fabrics include light- to medium-weight cotton, such as quilting cotton.

- ¼yd/23cm (or 1 fat quarter) of print fabric for the exterior and two dividers
- ⅛yd/11.5cm (or 1 fat quarter) of solid fabric for the exterior
- ¼yd/23cm (or 1 fat quarter) of coordinating print for the lining and one divider
- Template, page 105

ADDITIONAL SUPPLIES

- ¼yd/23cm of heavyweight fusible interfacing (see Fabric and Notions Source, page 123)
- Fabric marking pen
- 30"/76cm length of thick string, yarn, or jute
- Thread that matches the string, yarn, or jute (above), or invisible thread
- 6"/15cm twill tape or ribbon, 1"/2.5cm wide
- Zipper foot
- 1 zipper, 10"/25.5cm or longer

What You Do

CUT YOUR FABRIC

From the print fabric, cut:
- 2 upper panels, 3" × 10"/7.5cm × 25.5cm
- 2 dividers, 8" × 10"/20.5cm × 25.5cm

From the solid-color fabric, cut:
- 2 lower panels, 3½" × 10"/9cm × 25.5cm

From the coordinating print fabric, cut:
- 2 lining pieces, 6" × 10"/15cm × 25.5cm
- 1 divider, 8" × 10"/20.5cm × 25.5cm

From the interfacing, cut:
- 2 pieces, 6" × 10"/15cm × 25.5cm

PREPARE THE EXTERIOR

1 Stitch one upper and one lower panel piece, right sides together, along one long edge.

2 Press the seam allowance toward the upper panel and topstitch the seam (see Topstitching, page xii). Repeat with the remaining panel pieces.

3 Fuse the interfacing pieces to the back of each exterior piece. Set one exterior piece aside. Using A on page 105 and the fabric marking pen, transfer the word *save* to the right lower front panel of one exterior piece. Let the end of the letter *e* swing off the right side.

4 Place the string along the traced line at the beginning of the word and stitch it down with a zigzag stitch. Continue to follow the tracing with the string, zigzagging it in place until you reach the end. Keep the needle down as you pivot and turn. Remember to backstitch at the beginning and end.

TIP This technique is called couching. Be sure to use sewing machine thread that matches the color of your jute or yarn, or try invisible thread so it won't show at all.

PREPARE THE LINING

1 Cut the twill tape (or ribbon) into three pieces, each 2"/5cm long.

2 Fold a piece of twill tape in half and pin it to the center of the middle divider piece (the one that matches the lining) along what will become the top (10"/25.5cm edge), with raw edges even. Pin the remaining pieces of twill tape to the remaining dividers, one near the right edge and one near the left edge so the tabs will be staggered when the dividers are in the pouch (see B on page 105).

3 With right sides together, fold each divider piece in half by bringing the bottom edge to the top edge and sandwiching the tabs in between the layers. Stitch along the top edge only (see C on page 105.)

4 Turn the dividers right side out and press the seams flat. Topstitch along the seams.

5 Stack the dividers and place them on the right side of one of the lining pieces with the bottom edges of the dividers ⅜"/10mm above the bottom edge of the lining. Baste the side seams within the ¼"/6mm seam allowance (see Basting, page ix). (A)

INSERT THE ZIPPER

1 Install the zipper foot. Place the zipper right side up along the top, right side, edge of an exterior. Place a lining piece on top of the zipper with right side facing the zipper. Pin the exterior and lining to the zipper with all edges aligned and stitch in place (B).

2 Press the lining and exterior panels over so wrong sides are together and the zipper is exposed. Topstitch along the seam (see Topstitching, page xii).

> TIP If you would rather have the dividers caught in the bottom seam of the pouch, move them down so that they are aligned with the bottom edge of the lining before you baste the sides (see Basting, page ix).

> TIP I love using metal zippers, but extra care must be taken when sewing near the teeth. As you approach one end of a metal zipper, stop sewing with the foot pedal and use the hand wheel to slowly take each stitch. If your needle hits a metal part, wiggle the fabric until the needle slips in between or over the zipper teeth. Continue making each stitch with the hand wheel until you are past the zipper.

3 Repeat steps 1 and 2 above to stitch the remaining exterior and lining pieces to the other side of the zipper (C).

C

FINISH THE POUCH

1 Open up the zipper halfway and align the exterior pieces with the lining pieces, right sides together. Pin. Make sure the zipper teeth are pointing toward the exterior.

2 Stitch around the entire pouch, leaving a 5"/12.5cm opening in the lining for turning. Trim the corners and cut off the excess zipper tape using a pair of old scissors (D).

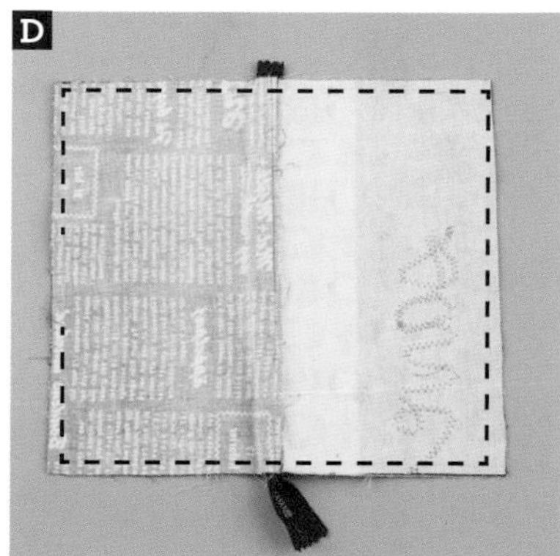
D

3 Turn the pouch right side out through the opening in the lining and sew the opening closed.

Take-Along Ironing Mats

Designed by Caroline Fairbanks-Critchfield

L LEVEL

This quick-to-sew, handy little mat can be made with ironing board fabric on one side plus heat resistant batting on the inside to protect the table underneath. Take it with you to sewing meet-ups, or use it to make a handy pressing station right at home. If you are able to use ironing board fabric for one side of the mat, it will reflect the heat of the iron and make pressing faster.

FINISHED SIZES 17" x 20"/43cm × 51cm (fat quarter-friendly size) 18" x 22"/45.5cm x 56cm (larger size)
SEAM ALLOWANCE Use ⅜"/10mm seam allowance, unless otherwise noted

What You Need

FABRIC

Suggested fabrics include 100% cotton for the top and bottom of the mat. Alternatively, reflective ironing board fabric may be used for the top of the mat.

For the fat quarter-friendly mat:

- 1 fat quarter (18" × 22"/45.5cm × 56cm cut of fabric) for the top
- 1 fat quarter (18" × 22"/45.5cm × 56cm cut of fabric) for the bottom

For the larger mat:

- ¾yd/68.5cm of fabric for the top
- ¾yd/68.5cm of fabric for the bottom

ADDITIONAL SUPPLIES

- 27"/68.5cm length of grosgrain ribbon, ½"-1"/13mm-2.5cm wide
- 1 fat quarter or ¾yd/68.5cm (depending on mat size) of insulated batting
- A chopstick or turning tool (if desired)
- Seam sealant (see Fabric and Notions Sources, page 123)

What You Do

CUT YOUR FABRIC

For the fat quarter-friendly mat:
From each fat quarter (top and bottom), cut:

- 1 piece 18" × 21"/45.5cm × 53.5cm

From the insulated batting, cut:

- 1 piece 17½" × 20½"/44.5cm × 52cm

For the larger mat:
From each fabric (top and bottom), cut:

- 1 piece 19" × 23"/48.5cm × 58.5cm

From the insulated batting, cut:

- 1 piece 18½" × 22½"/47cm × 57cm

MAKE THE IRONING MAT

1 Cut the grosgrain ribbon in half. Center (top to bottom) one piece of ribbon on each side of the top or bottom fabric piece, as shown. Baste in place (see Basting, page ix). (A)

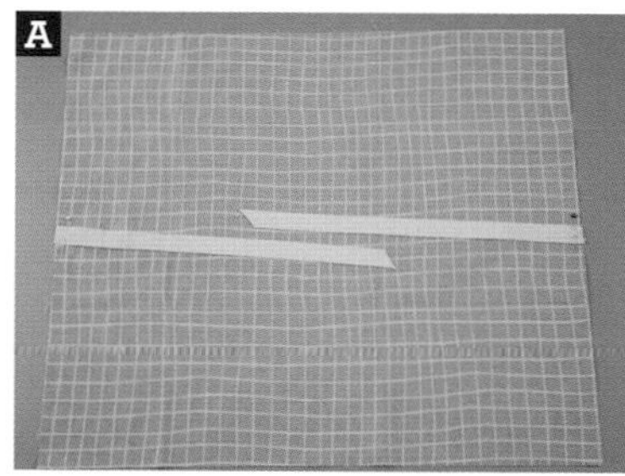
A

2 Layer the top and bottom fabrics, right sides together, with the ribbon sandwiched in between. Lay the insulated batting on top and pin around all edges (B).

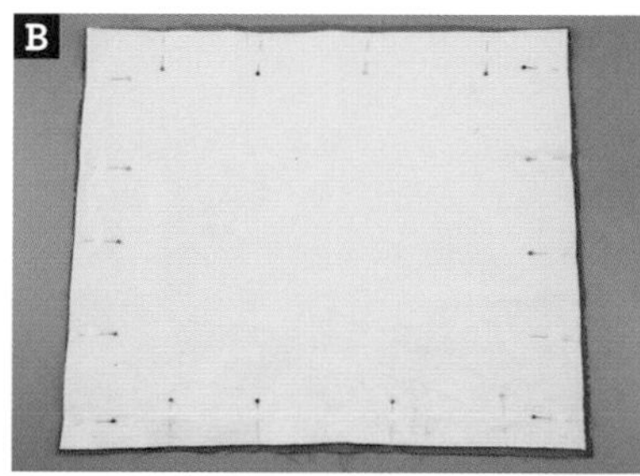
B

3 Stitch around the mat, pivoting at the corners. Leave a 5"/12.5cm opening on one edge for turning.

4 Trim the corners. Turn the mat right side out and press. Use a chopstick or turning tool if necessary to push the corners out. Fold the open edges to the inside and press. Hand-sew the opening closed (see Slip Stitching, page xi). (C)

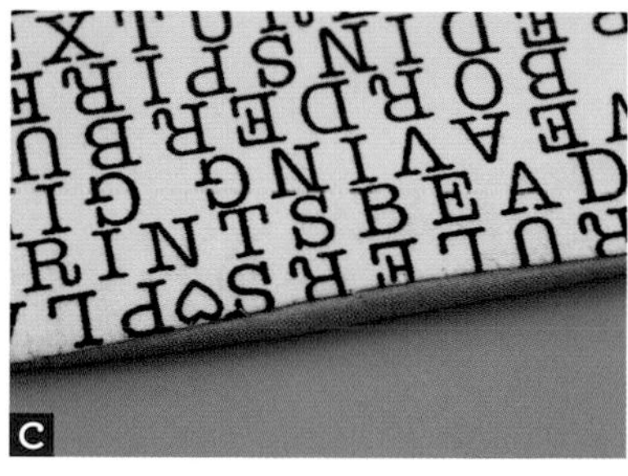
C

5 Trim the ribbon ends into points, if desired. Seal the raw edges of the ribbon with the seam sealant.

6 Fold the longer (top and bottom) edges toward the center, in thirds. Then fold the mat in half, bringing the ribbon pieces together and tie.

4 5 6 7
60in/150cm

Snappy Supply Case

Designed by Becky Jorgensen

LEVEL

This cute case has a pincushion, needle keeper, and scissor holder, and the see-through vinyl pockets are perfect for a little work in progress. You'll love the snappy closures, and the hand-stitched accessory holders keep your sewing tools safe. Whether your favorite craft is sewing, knitting, crochet, or something else, this case will hold exactly what you need.

FINISHED SIZE Approximately 10½" × 7"/26.5cm × 18cm closed
SEAM ALLOWANCE Use ¼"/6mm seam allowance, unless otherwise noted

What You Need

FABRIC

- Suggested fabrics include light- to medium-weight cotton (quilting fabrics) and cotton blends.
- ½yd/45.5cm (or 2 fat quarters) of main fabric
- ¼yd/23cm (or 1 fat quarter) of accent fabric
- ¼yd/23cm (or 1 fat quarter) of fabric for the binding and large strap
- Scraps of fabric for the scissor holder and pincushion
- Scrap of wool felt for the needle keeper, 2" × 5"/5cm × 12.5cm

ADDITIONAL SUPPLIES

- ½yd/45.5cm of thin quilt batting
- 1 small and one medium-size button (approx. ¾" and ⅜" in diameter)
- 1yd/91cm of lightweight vinyl*
- Tiny amount of polyester stuffing for the pincushion
- Crewel needle and embroidery floss
- 1 sew-on snap
- 4 pieces cut from a heavy-duty metal tape measure, each 9"/23cm long (and heavy-duty scissors to cut them)
- 16"/40.5cm length of ⅜"/10mm or ¼"/6mm wide grosgrain ribbon for the pocket pulls
- Double-sided sewing adhesive (see Fabric and Notions Sources, page 123) or double-sided tape
- Fabric marking pen

What You Do

CUT YOUR FABRIC

From the main fabric, cut:

- 2 outer case pieces, 10½" × 14"/26.5cm × 35.5cm

From the accent fabric, cut:

- 1 binding strip, 2" × 10½"/5cm × 26.5cm
- 4 measuring tape casings, 5½" × 10"/14cm × 25.5cm

From the binding fabric, cut:

- 2 strips, 2"/5cm × width of fabric (cut off the selvages)**
- 2 strips, 2½" × 7"/6.5cm × 18cm for the large strap

From the scraps of fabric, cut:

- 1 pincushion, 4" × 6"/10cm × 15cm
- 1 scissor holder, 6" × 6"/15cm × 15cm
- 1 scissor holder strap, 2" × 3½"/5cm × 9cm

From the scrap of wool felt, cut:

- 1 needle keeper, 2" × 5"/5cm × 12.5cm

From the vinyl, cut:

- 1 side pocket, 4½" × 10½"/11.5cm × 26.5cm
- 2 pockets, 10" × 10"/25.5cm × 25.5cm

From the quilt batting, cut:

- 1 outer casing piece, 10½" × 14"/26.5cm × 35.5cm
- 1 large strap, 2½" × 7"/6.5cm × 18cm

From the grosgrain ribbon, cut:

- 4 pieces, each 4"/10cm long

PREPARE THE OUTER CASE AND STRAP

1 Sandwich the large piece of quilt batting between the two main fabric pieces with the right side of the fabrics facing out. Quilt the layers together in straight lines or in any design you prefer (see Straight Line Quilting, page xi). (A)

* Lightweight vinyl can be purchased in the home decorating department of most fabric stores, but you might also try repurposing other vinyl such as the bag that your sheets or bedspread came in.

** If you are using a fat quarter, cut four strips 2" x 20"/5cm x 51cm (or the width of the fat quarter) and sew them together to make two strips approximately 2" x 40"/5cm x 101.5cm.

2 Pin the strap pieces right sides together, with the remaining piece of quilt batting on the bottom. Stitch around all the sides, leaving a 3"/7.5cm opening for turning on one long edge (B).

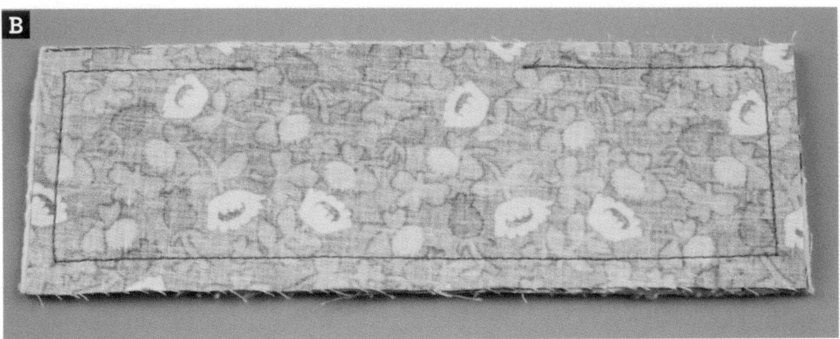

3 Trim the corners and trim the batting close to the stitching. Turn the strap right side out through the opening. Press the strap flat, pressing the raw edges ¼"/6mm to the inside. Topstitch around the strap (see Topstitching, page xii), closing the opening as you go.

4 Make a buttonhole on one end of the strap, centered and ½"/13mm from the end. Make it long enough that the larger button fits through it.

5 Mark the middle of the strap. Center and pin the strap to the outside (and back) of the case so the middle of the strap aligns with the outside edge of the case, as shown. Stitch the strap in place 1"/2.5cm from the outside edge of the case and again 2½"/6.5cm from the outside edge (C).

PREPARE AND ATTACH THE SIDE POCKET

1 Press the binding strip, cut from the accent fabric (2" × 10½"/5cm × 26.5cm), as directed in Pressing Bias and Straight Binding and Other Fabric Strips (page ix).

2 Wrap the binding around one long edge of the smaller piece of vinyl. Secure with sewing clips, if needed.

3 Topstitch the binding to the vinyl close to the pressed folds of the binding (see Topstitching, page xii).

TIPS FOR SEWING WITH VINYL

- Never use straight pins. If you need to secure fabric to the vinyl, use sewing clips or double-sided tape.
- Lengthen the stitch length to reduce the amount of perforation of the vinyl.
- Using a warm iron to soften and smooth out wrinkles is fine, but always use a press cloth between the iron and the vinyl.

4 Fold the case in half and mark the middle at the top and the bottom edges. Lay the side pocket inside the case so the bottom (unbound) edge abuts the middle marking and the pocket extends across the back. Secure with clips.

Note: The side pocket should be on the same end of the case as the large strap. Keep in mind, however, that the strap is on the outside and the side pocket is on the inside.

5 Baste the side pocket to the sides of the case (see Basting, page ix).

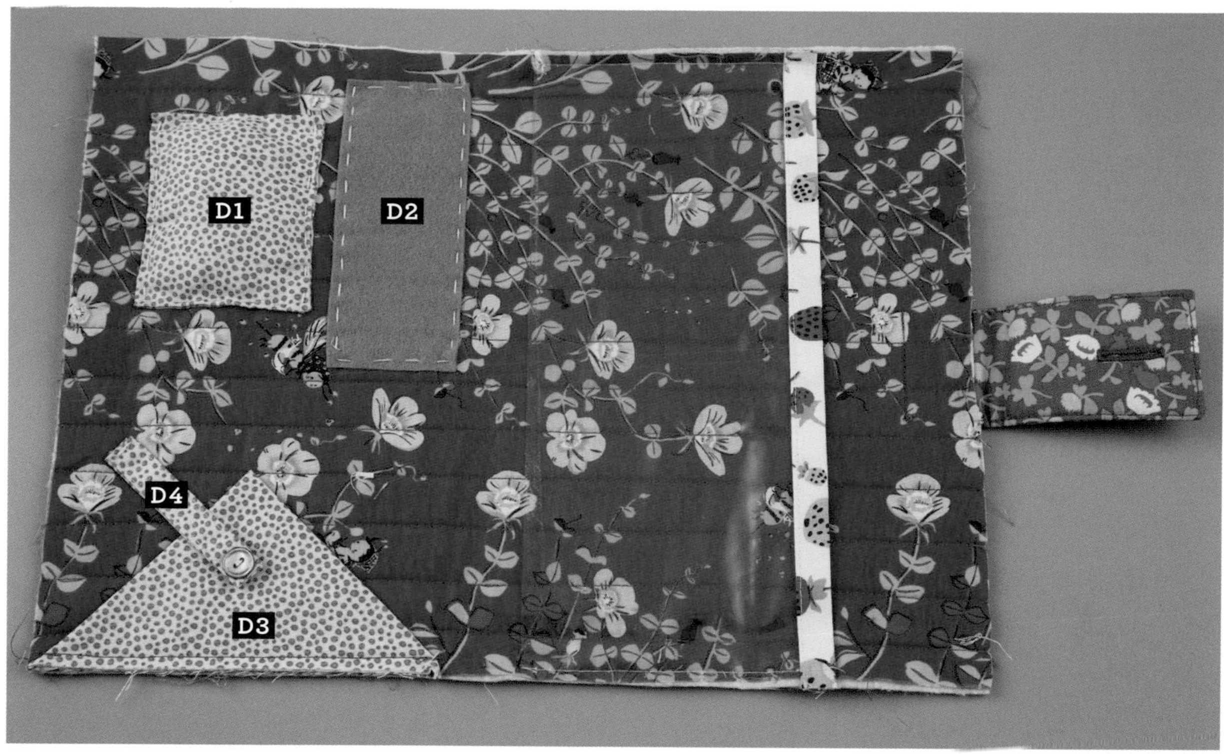

PREPARE AND ATTACH THE PINCUSHION, NEEDLE KEEPER, AND SCISSOR HOLDER

The pincushion, needle keeper, and scissor holder all are attached to the inside front of the case, opposite the vinyl side pocket.

1 Fold the pincushion piece in half wrong sides together to make a 4" × 3"/10cm × 7.5cm rectangle. Stitch around the three open sides, leaving a 2"/5cm opening for stuffing.

2 Trim the corners, turn the pincushion right side out, and press the raw edges to the inside. Stuff very lightly with polyester fiberfill.

3 Pin the edges of the pincushion to the case interior approximately 1½"/4cm from the top edge and 1"/2.5cm from the left side. If it is difficult to pin the pincushion down, remove some polyester fiberfill. You only need a tiny bit.

4 Using the needle and embroidery thread, hand-sew the pincushion to the case around all four sides, ⅛"/3mm from the edge. Use long running stitches and take care not to let your stitches show on the outside of the case (D1).

5 Pin the piece of wool felt ¼"/6mm away from the pincushion so it is vertical and approximately ¾"/2cm away from the top of the case. Hand-sew it in place ⅛"/3mm from the edge with embroidery thread, just as you did with the pincushion (D2).

6 With wrong sides together, fold the scissor-holder piece in half diagonally twice to form a triangle and press. Pin the long raw edges to the bottom edge. The point of the triangle should point to the inside of the case. Baste it in place ¼"/6mm from the bottom edge (see Basting, page ix). (D3)

7 Press the narrow ends of the scissor-holder strap ¼"/6mm to the wrong side. Then press the long edges of the strip as directed in Pressing Bias and Straight Grain Binding and Other Fabric Strips (pages ix and x). Topstitch around all sides ⅛"/3mm from the edge to make a ½" x 3"/13mm x 7.5cm strap (see Topstitching, page xii).

8 On one end of the strap, hand-sew half of the snap on one side and the small button on the other side.

9 Hand-sew the end of the strap without the button to the inside of the case, as pictured. Sew the opposite side of the snap to the fabric triangle so that the strap will lie flat over the triangle and hold the scissors in place (D4).

MAKE AND ATTACH THE SNAPPY POCKETS

Review the tips for sewing with vinyl (page 34) before you start.

1 Press all the metal tape measure casings in half lengthwise, wrong sides together.

2 Align the long raw edges of a pressed casing piece against one side of a vinyl square and stitch. Repeat on the opposite side of the square. Sew the remaining casing pieces to the remaining vinyl square in the same way (E).

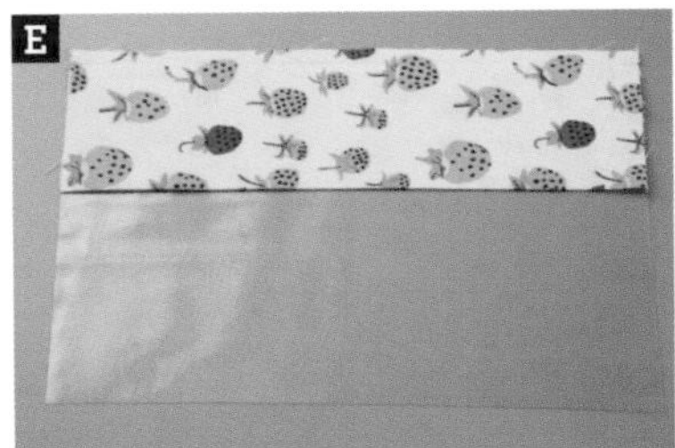

3 Finger-press the casing away from the vinyl. Mark the center of the casings for the ribbon pulls.

4 Wrap and fold the casing over to the opposite side of the vinyl so the casing fold just covers the seam. Pin along the edge, through the fabric only.

5 Topstitch the casing to the vinyl (see Topstitching, page xii), stopping just before the halfway mark. Slide one end of a 4"/10cm ribbon under the casing. Continue stitching to secure the ribbon end and then insert the other end of the ribbon to form the pocket pull (F).

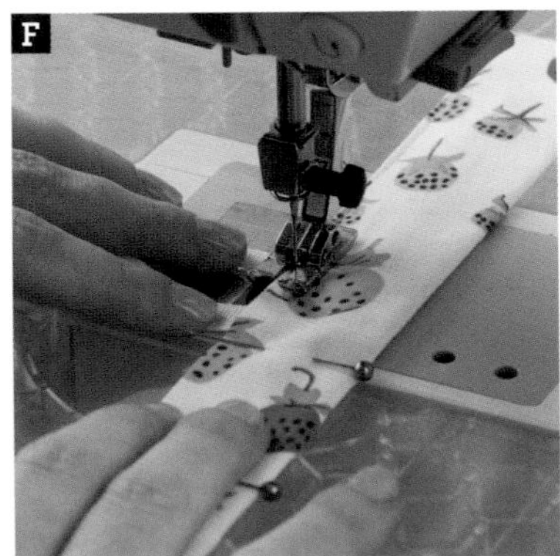

6 Repeat steps 2–5 to finish all the casings.

7 Place the two vinyl pocket pieces together so the ribbon pulls are facing each other and stitch along one side. Use pins on the fabric ends only and clips on the vinyl, if needed (G).

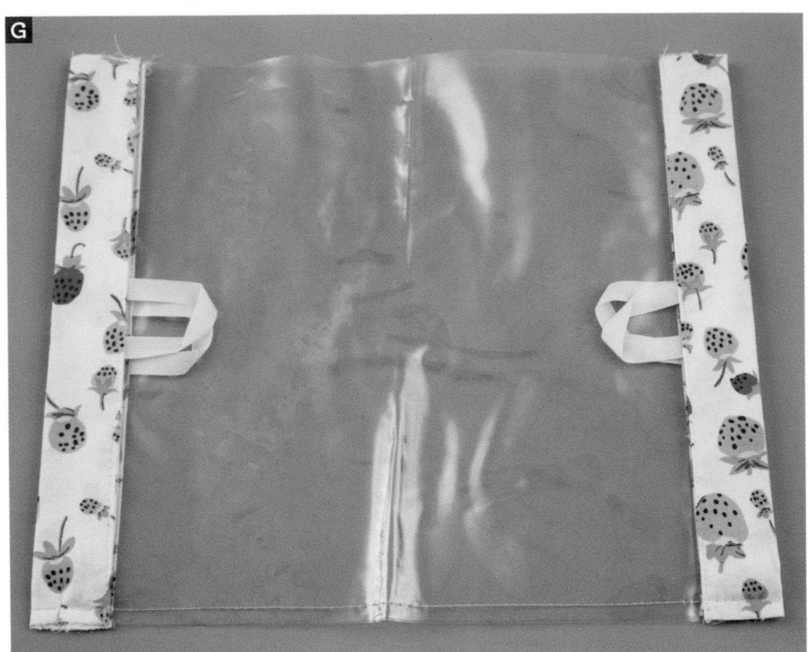

8 Using a heavy-duty scissors, round the ends of the metal tape measure pieces. (This will help them to slide smoothly through the casings and keep them from poking holes in the casing later.)

9 Insert the curved tape measure pieces into the middle of the casings so the bowed-out sides are on the same side as the ribbon pulls. Push them as far into the casings as they will go (H).

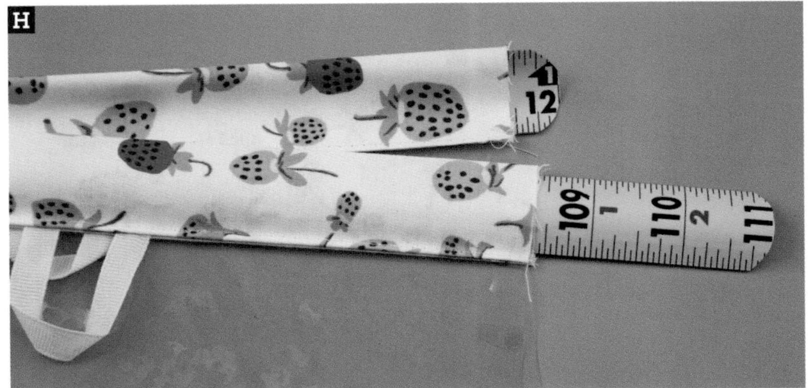

10 Stitch the remaining open side of the vinyl pockets, right sides together. Turn the vinyl pocket right side out (so the seam allowances are on the inside).

11 Apply a strip of double-sided sewing adhesive or double-sided tape down the middle of the case interior to align with the unfinished edge of the side pocket. Center the snappy pocket piece over the adhesive and press to adhere.

12 Cut a 10½"/26.5cm length from one of the binding strips cut from the binding fabric. Press each long edge ½"/13mm to the wrong side, so it is 1"/2.5cm wide. Position it over the center of the snappy pocket, covering the adhesive and the unbound edge of the side pocket. Pin it in place through the fabric and not through visible vinyl (I).

TIP It's easy to turn the vinyl pocket without too much trouble. Soften up both sides by placing the entire piece under a press cloth and gently applying a warm iron. Then turn the snap closure on one end to the inside. Reach through from the other end and pull it out gently.

13 Stitch the binding in place, through all the layers, along both long edges.

FINISH

This case is bound in one step, differently than other projects in this book. If you would prefer to bind in two steps, refer to the method shown for the Spacious Spa Caddy (page 55).

1 Stitch the binding fabric strips together to make one continuous strip and press, as directed in Pressing Bias and Straight Binding and Other Fabric Strips (page ix).

2 Starting in an inconspicuous area, wrap the binding strip around the edge of the case. Stitch the binding to the case exterior, close to the folded edge. Go slowly, checking to make sure that the binding is caught on the opposite (underneath) side.

3 To miter the corners, stitch all the way to the corner, stop stitching, raise the needle, and cut your threads. Fold the binding down at a 90-degree angle, and then wrap it around to the next side. Insert the needle, backstitch neatly, and continue stitching. Repeat for all four corners (J, K, L).

J

K

L

4 Once you reach the starting point, trim away all except 1"/2.5cm of extra binding. Fold the raw edges under, and sew the end down covering the beginning raw edge of the binding (M).

M

5 Close the case and wrap the large strap around to the front. Mark the spot for the button and hand-sew it in place.

TIP If you enjoy using the snappy closure on this project, check out the "Snappy Coin Purse" free tutorial on my blog, SewCanShe.com. It uses tape measure pieces, too.

WESTCOTT
MADE IN U.S.A.

Crafty Biz Apron

Designed by Caroline Fairbanks-Critchfield

LEVEL

Sell (or sew) your crafty items in style with this cute and clever vendor apron. The sizes of the front pockets are customizable to suit your needs and there's even a hidden zipper pocket for stashing away money. Variations include regular or long ties (the long ties are for tying in front) and an optional swivel clip for hanging keys or a small pair of scissors.

FINISHED SIZE 12" long × 24" wide/30.5cm x 61cm, not including the ties

SEAM ALLOWANCE Use ½"/13mm seam allowance, unless otherwise noted

What You Need

FABRIC

Suggested fabrics include light- to medium-weight wovens, such as cotton shirting or quilting cotton.

- 1yd/91cm of main fabric for the apron lining/front pockets and waistband/ties
- ¾yd/68.5cm of coordinating fabric for the panel above the pockets and the hidden pocket

ADDITIONAL SUPPLIES

- Fabric marking pen
- Acrylic ruler
- Chopstick or turning tool
- Double-sided adhesive, if desired
- 1 zipper, at least 8"/20.5cm long
- Zipper foot
- Swivel snap clip with a 1"/2.5cm strap opening (optional), if desired, for holding keys or scissors

What You Do

CUT YOUR FABRIC

From the main fabric, cut:

- 1 apron lining/front pocket piece, 19" × 25"/48.5cm × 63.5cm
- 3 waistband/ties pieces 5" × 40"/12.5cm × 101.5cm for tie ends that wrap around and tie in the front or 5" × 30"/12.5cm × 76cm for regular-length tie ends that tie in the back
- 1 tab 4"/10cm square for the optional key or scissors holder

From the coordinating fabric, cut:

- 1 apron front, 19" × 25"/48.5cm × 63.5cm
- 1 hidden pocket piece, 13" × 10"/33cm × 25.5cm

MAKE THE HIDDEN ZIPPER POCKET

1 Draw a ½" × 8"/13mm × 20.5cm rectangle on the wrong side of the hidden pocket piece, 1¼"/3cm down from the top edge and 1"/2.5cm away from the side edges, as shown in A on page 106. Using an acrylic ruler, draw a horizontal line through the center of the rectangle and connect this line to the corners with a little triangle at each end, as shown in A on page 106.

2 With right sides together, center and pin the hidden pocket piece to the top edge of the apron front, as shown in A on page 106.

3 Sew around the ½" x 8"/13mm x 20.5cm rectangle drawn on the wrong side of the hidden pocket piece (A).

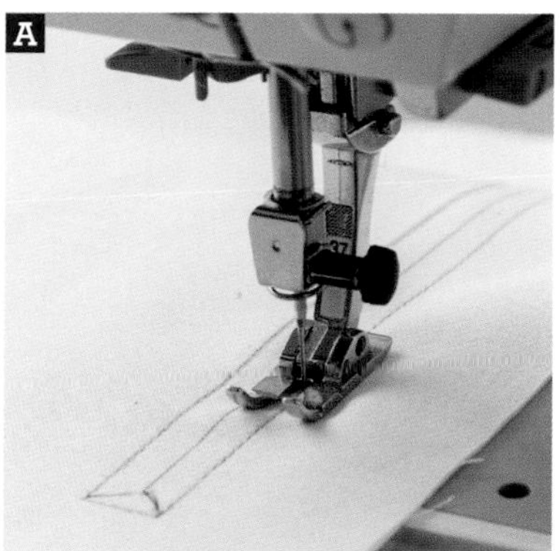
A

4 Cut along the line in the center of the rectangle and cut out to the corners without cutting through the stitching. Push the pocket piece through the opening to the wrong side and press (B).

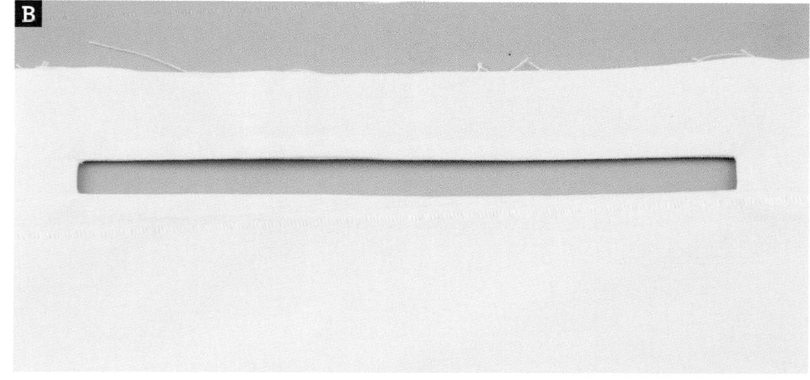
B

5 Apply pieces of double-sided sewing adhesive to the zipper tapes (C).

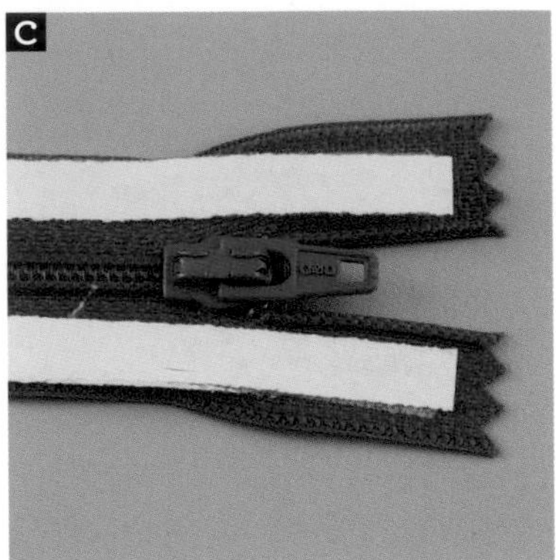
C

6 Remove the remaining paper from the adhesive. Center the zipper underneath the pocket so it appears in the opening and finger-press to temporarily stick the zipper in place. Make sure the zipper pull is visible through the slot.

Note: If you are not using double-sided sewing adhesive, simply pin the zipper in place instead.

7 Install the zipper foot on your sewing machine. Topstitch around the opening, close to the edges to secure the zipper (see Topstitching, page xii). (D)

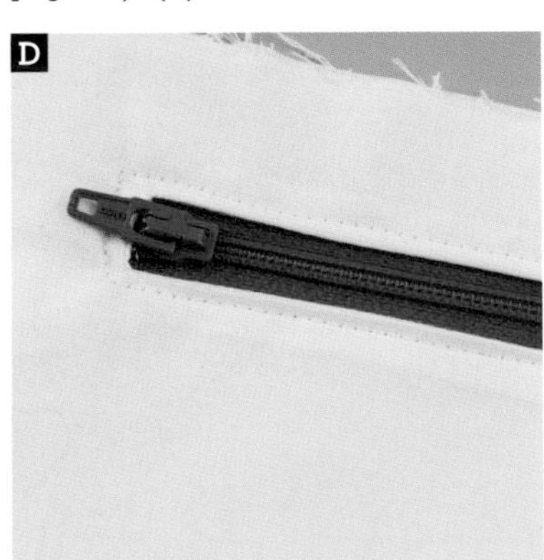
D

8 Fold the pocket piece in half over the back of the zipper so the raw edges are aligned at the top of the apron front. Pin and stitch the sides of the pocket together. The top edge will be caught in the apron seam (E).

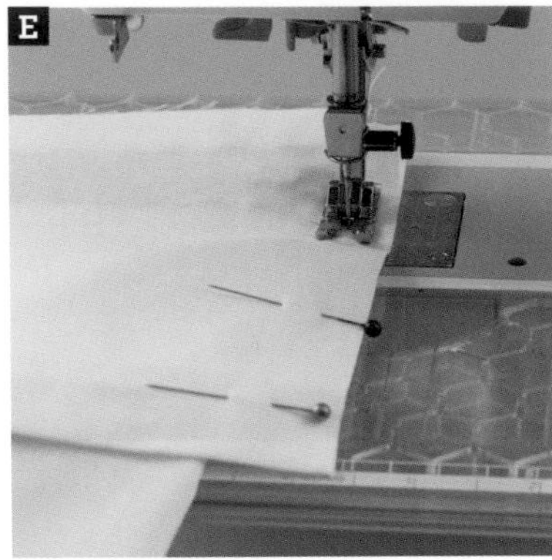
E

MAKE THE APRON

1 With the right sides together, pin the apron front to the lining/front pocket (both 19" × 25"/48.5cm × 63.5cm).

2 Stitch all the way around, catching the top of the hidden pocket in the stitching. Leave a 4"/10cm break in the stitching along the bottom edge for turning (see B on page 106).

3 Trim the corners. Remove some of the bulk from the top seam by separating the layers and trimming the pocket seam allowance to ¼"/6mm.

4 Turn the apron right side out. Push out the corners and straight edges with the turning tool. Press the apron flat and the raw edges of the opening to the inside.

5 Topstitch along the bottom edge (see Topstitching, page xii), closing the opening as you go (F).

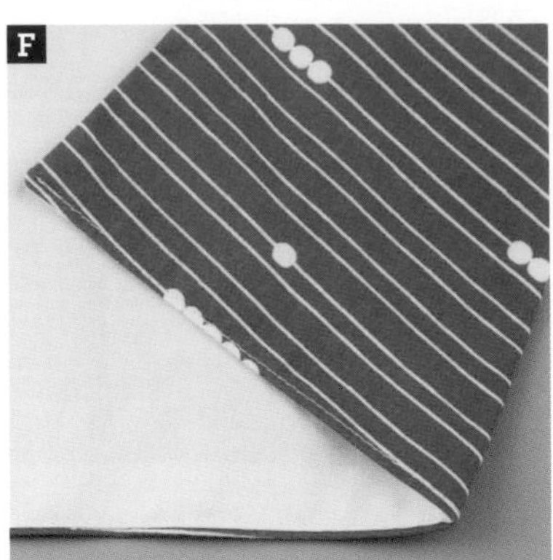
F

TIP Topstitch with your lining/front pocket fabric facing up. It will soon show on the front.

6 Fold the bottom of the apron 6"/15cm to the right side so the lining/pocket fabric is visible on the right side of the apron; pin along the sides. Stitch the entire length of the sides, through all the layers, ⅛"/3mm from the edge.

7 Measure and mark any size pockets with the fabric marking pen and ruler. I suggest three main pockets, approximately 6"/15cm wide and three pen or pencil pockets approximately 2"/5cm wide. Stitch along the marked lines, backstitching neatly at the top and bottom of each pocket (see C on page 107).

MAKE THE WAISTBAND AND TIES

The waistband and ties are one piece. The center portion becomes the waistband while the sides become the ties.

1 Stitch the three waistband/ties pieces together to make one long strip. Press the seams open.

2 Fold the waistband/ties piece in half lengthwise with the right sides together, and stitch around the long and short edges, leaving a 4"/10cm opening for turning.

3 Trim the corners. Use the chopstick or turning tool to turn the piece right side out and to push out the corners. Turn the raw edges to the inside and press.

4 Center the waistband/ties along the top edge and right side of the apron, covering the hidden zipper pocket opening. Pin along the top edge (see D on page 107).

5 Stitch the waistband to the apron ⅛"/3mm from the top edge. Continue sewing to topstitch around one tie. After topstitching around the tie, do not stitch the bottom edge of the waistband to the apron. Move the apron out of the way so you can topstitch the bottom edge of the waistband and then topstitch around the other tie. Backstitch when you reach the place where you started sewing.

6 Stitch the waistband down along both side edges of the apron.

MAKE TAB FOR KEYS OR SCISSORS

1 Fold the 4"/10cm tab piece in half, wrong sides together, and press. Unfold the piece. Then fold the edges to the center fold line and press again. Fold the piece in half again to make a 1" × 4"/2.5cm × 10cm tab and press. See Pressing Bias and Straight Binding and Other Fabric Strips (page xii).

2 Topstitch close to both long edges of the tab (see Topstitching, page xii).

3 Slip the tab on the swivel snap clip and zigzag the raw edges of the tab together (G).

4 Insert the tab edges ½"/13mm under the waistband 1"/2.5cm away from the left side (this will be the right side when you're wearing the apron). Sew along the bottom of the waistband (through all layers) from the left edge for 2"/5cm, just enough to secure the tab.

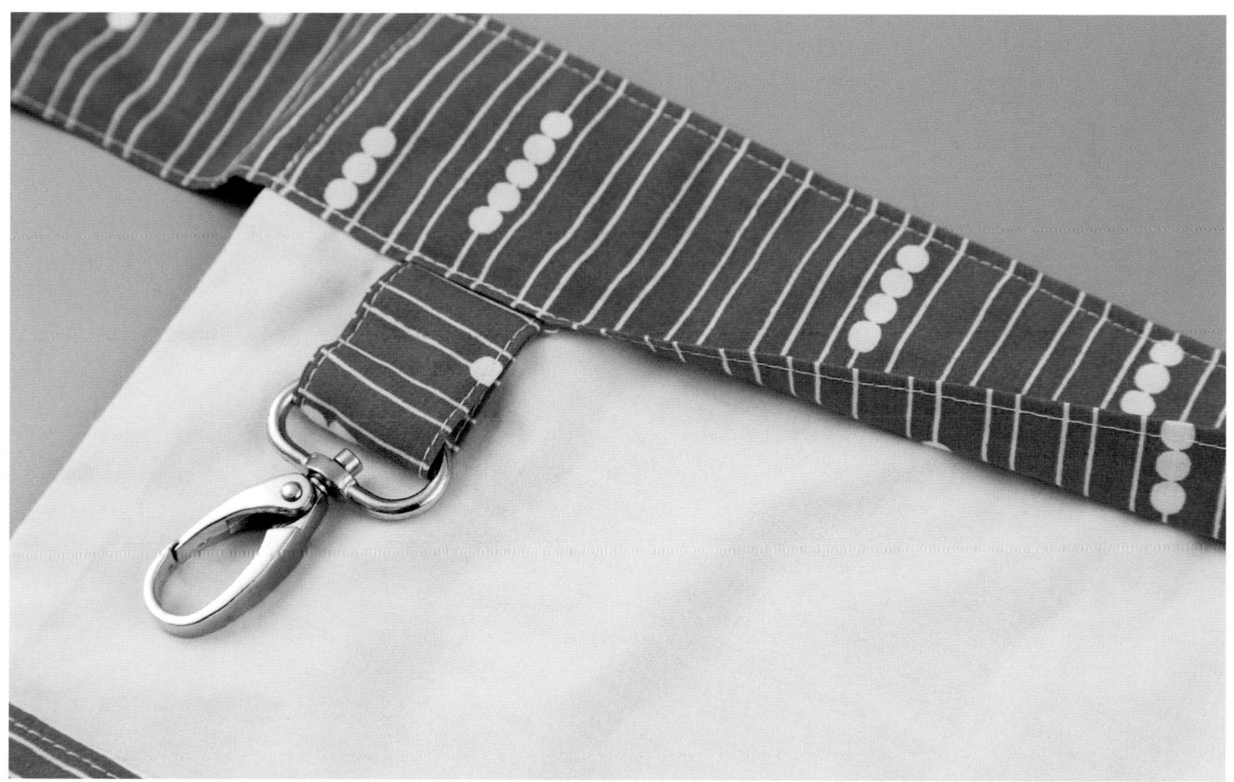

Where you stumble and fall,
there you discover gold.

So functional and fun to make, these household items will hone your sewing skills and bring beauty and comfort to your daily routines.

FAT QUARTER friendly!

Reversible Barstool Cushion

Designed by Caroline Fairbanks-Critchfield

L LEVEL ● ●

This sweet little cushion is perfect for a barstool with a back or for a medium-sized chair. Floral and striped fabrics make a fun combination—simply flip the cushion over to create a whole new look for your room. Customize the cushion further with contrasting fabric for the piping, if you wish.

FINISHED SIZE Approximately 15" long x 16" wide x 2–3" thick/38cm x 40.5cm x 5–7.5cm, not including the ties

SEAM ALLOWANCE Use ½"/13mm seam allowance, unless otherwise noted

What You Need

Suggested fabrics include medium-weight wovens, such as quilting cotton, cotton/linen blends, and home décor fabrics.

FABRIC

- ½yd/45.5cm of decorative fabric (or 1 fat quarter) for the top
- ½yd/45.5cm of fabric (or 1 fat quarter) for the bottom
- ¼yd/23cm of fabric (or 1 fat quarter) for the piping
- ¼yd/23cm of coordinating fabric (or 1 fat quarter) for the ties and buttons
- Template, page 108

ADDITIONAL SUPPLIES

- ½yd/45.5cm of polyester quilt batting
- Fabric basting spray
- 2yd/1.8m of ¼"/6mm-diameter cotton filler cord
- Zipper foot
- Polyester fiberfill
- Covered button kit, 1⅛"/2.9cm-diameter (size 45) buttons, or other coordinating buttons
- Fabric marking pen
- Long needle and strong thread for hand sewing

What You Do

CUT THE FABRIC

Using the pattern found on page 108, cut:

- 1 top from decorative fabric
- 1 bottom from decorative fabric
- 2 pieces of quilt batting

TIP You can also customize this cushion to fit your barstool or chair perfectly. Instead of printing the included pattern, lay a large sheet of paper over the seat of your barstool or chair and trace the shape. Remove the paper and add 1½"/4cm to all edges of the traced seat to account for the seam allowance and the cushion filling. Cut out your custom pattern and follow the instructions as written, except that your pieces will not be cut out on the fold.

From the piping fabric, cut:

- 2"/5cm-wide bias strips, as described in Making Bias Binding (page ix).

From the coordinating fabric, cut:

- 4 ties, 3" × 18"/7.5cm × 45.5cm
- 2 circles for the covered buttons

PREPARE THE FABRIC

1 Use the fabric basting spray to attach the batting pieces to the wrong side of the cushion top and bottom pieces.

2 Join the bias strips to make at least 60"/152.5cm of continuous bias binding as described in Making Bias Binding (page ix).

MAKE AND ATTACH THE PIPING

1 Fold the bias strip in half, wrong sides together, and place the cotton filler cord inside the fold for several inches (about 7–10cm). This will now be referred to as piping.

2 Pin the end of the piping to the right side of the cushion top at the center back marking (as indicated on the pattern piece). Align the raw edges of the piping with the raw edge of the cushion piece (A).

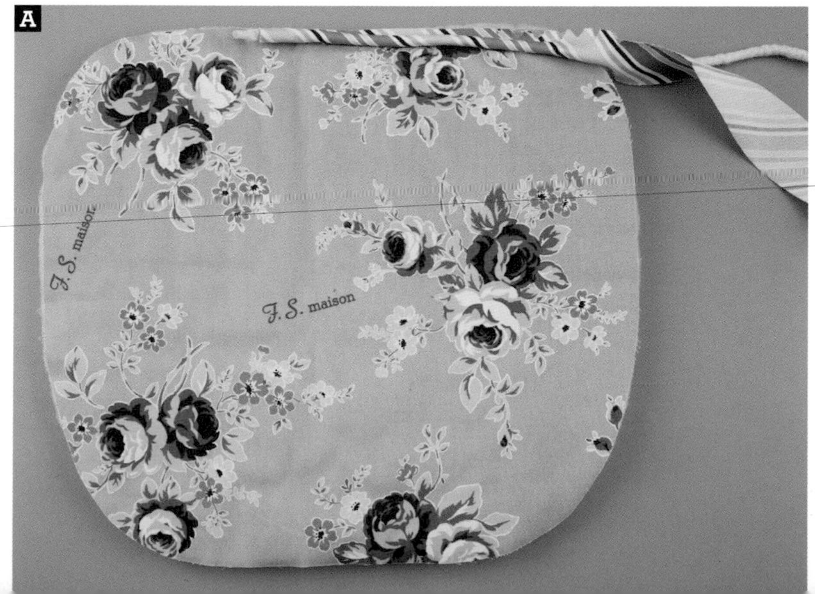

3 Attach the zipper foot to your sewing machine. Begin stitching about 2"/5cm from the beginning end of the piping and as close to the filler cord as possible. As you stitch, feed the filler cord into the center of the bias trim. Make ½"/13mm clips into the bias tape (see Clipping and Notching, page x), up to but not through, the stitching to ease the piping around the corners (B).

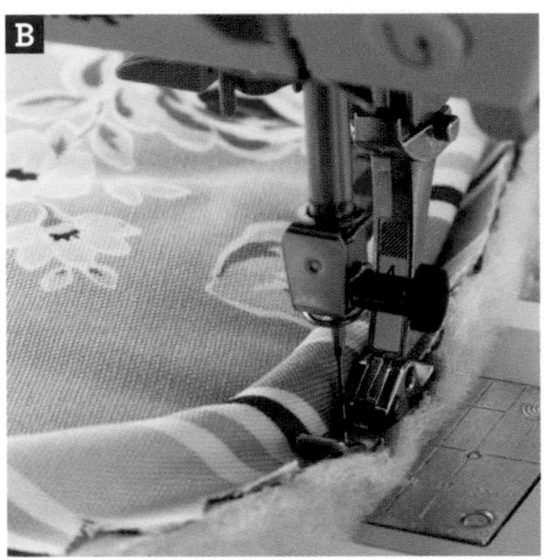

4 When you are a few inches/7-10cm away from the center back, stop and cut the filler cord inside the piping so the ends of the filler cord abut, but don't overlap. You may need to trim the filler cord from the start of the seam, too. Angle both ends of the piping off the cushion back and finish sewing it to the cushion (C).

MAKE AND ATTACH THE TIES

1 Fold and press the tie strips, as directed in Pressing Bias and Straight Binding and Other Fabric Strips (page ix).

2 Topstitch ⅛"/3mm from both long edges of the ties (see Topstitching, page xii).

3 Stitch one end of each tie to the bottom cushion piece at the back corners, as indicated on the pattern piece (D).

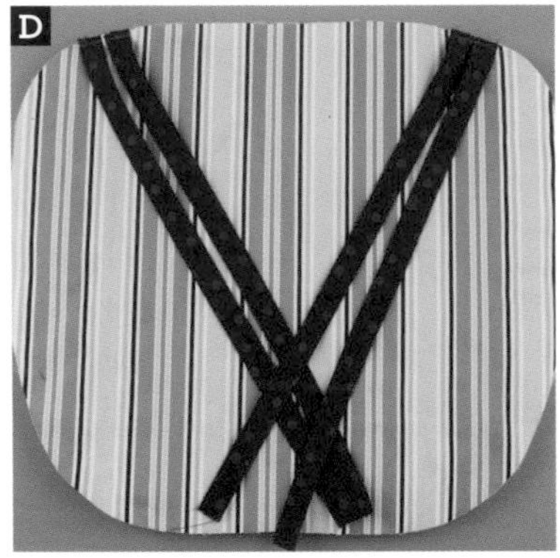

SEW THE CUSHION

1 Pin the cushion top and bottom pieces with right sides together and the piping and ties sandwiched in between (E).

2 Stitch around the cushion, sewing on top of the stitching that attached the piping to the top piece. Use the zipper foot so you can sew close to the filler cord again. Leave a 6"/15cm opening at the back for turning.

3 Turn the cushion right side out through the opening and gently steam-press. Insert polyester fiberfill to stuff the cushion to the desired thickness. Distribute the fiberfill evenly. Hand-sew the opening closed (F).

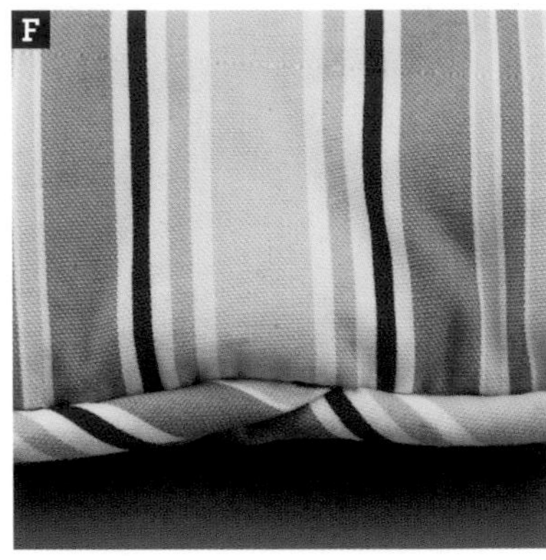

ATTACH THE BUTTONS

1 Prepare two covered buttons following the manufacturer's instructions (or use your own coordinating buttons). Mark the center of the cushion on the top and the bottom. Refer to the pattern piece, if needed.

2 Thread a long needle with the strong thread. Insert the needle through the mark on the cushion, center top to the center bottom. Take a small stitch and push the needle through to the top again. Tie the thread ends tightly (G).

3 Sew one covered button to the cushion top and then push the needle through to the cushion bottom. Attach the remaining button. Tie a knot and hide the thread ends inside the cushion.

4 Attach the cushion to the barstool or chair using the ties. Cut the ties shorter, if desired. Fold the tie ends over ¼"/6mm twice and stitch close to the fold.

Everyday Apron

Designed by Caroline Fairbanks-Critchfield

LEVEL

Take a yard/meter of your favorite fabric, whip up some coordinating bias binding to go around it, and this apron will be the one you want to wear every day. Optional pockets make it even more useful.

FINISHED SIZE Approximately 32" wide x 30" long/81cm x 76cm, not including the ties
SEAM ALLOWANCE No seam allowance required for this project

What You Need

FABRIC

Suggested fabrics include medium-weight wovens, such as quilting cotton, cotton-linen blends, and home décor fabrics.

- 1yd/91cm of main fabric for the apron
- ½yd/45.5cm of coordinating fabric for the bias binding and pockets
- Templates, page 109

ADDITIONAL SUPPLIES

- Fabric marking pen

What You Do

CUT YOUR FABRIC

From the main fabric, cut one piece, 32" wide × 30" long/81cm × 76cm. Fold the piece in half lengthwise and use the "Fabric Layout for Apron Body" template (A on page 109) and the fabric marking pen to mark an inward curve at the top of the apron and an outward curve at the bottom of the apron, as shown. Cut along the marked lines through both layers.

From the coordinating fabric, mark and cut two pockets, using the "Fabric Layout for Pockets" template (B on page 109).

Also from the coordinating fabric, cut 2"/5cm-wide bias strips as described in Making Bias Binding (page ix). Join the strips to make 6 yd/5.5m of bias binding or see note on page 52.

MAKE AND ATTACH THE POCKETS

1 Sew around the sides and bottom edges of the pockets, ½"/13mm from the edge. This helps ease the fabric around the curves. Press the edges to the back along the stitching line. Use a pin to gently pull the stitches in the corners so that the edges gather slightly and fold over neatly.

2 Press the top straight edge of the pockets to the back ½"/13mm and then ½"/13mm again. Sew along the inside folded edge (A).

A

3 Arrange the pockets on the front of the apron. (I placed mine about 5½"/14cm away from the side and curved edges.) When you are happy with your pocket placement, pin them in place and stitch around the side and bottom edges (B).

B

PRESS AND ATTACH THE BIAS BINDING

1 Fold and press the bias binding as directed in Pressing Bias and Straight Binding and Other Fabric Strips (page ix).

2 Cut a 10"/25.5cm piece of bias binding. Wrap it around the top edge of the apron and pin. Sew the binding about ⅛"/3mm from the fold. Make sure you catch the binding on both sides of the apron (C).

Note: If you don't want to make your own bias binding, you can substitute 2 packages of double-fold, extra-wide bias tape from any sewing or craft store.

3 Starting at the lower corner on the right side (near the pocket), wrap the binding over the fabric edge, down the right side, around the bottom curved edge, and up the opposite side. Pin. Cut away the extra binding. Stitch the binding ⅛"/3m from the fold.

4 Cut the remaining binding in half to make two pieces, each approximately 68–70 inches/172.5–178cm long. Measure 20"/51cm from one end of each binding piece and make a mark (D).

5 Pin the binding pieces around the remaining (armhole) curved edges. The marks that are 20"/51cm from one end of each piece should be placed at the top corners of the apron. This will make 20"/51cm-long ties at the top and about 30"/76cm-long ties at each side edge (see opposite page).

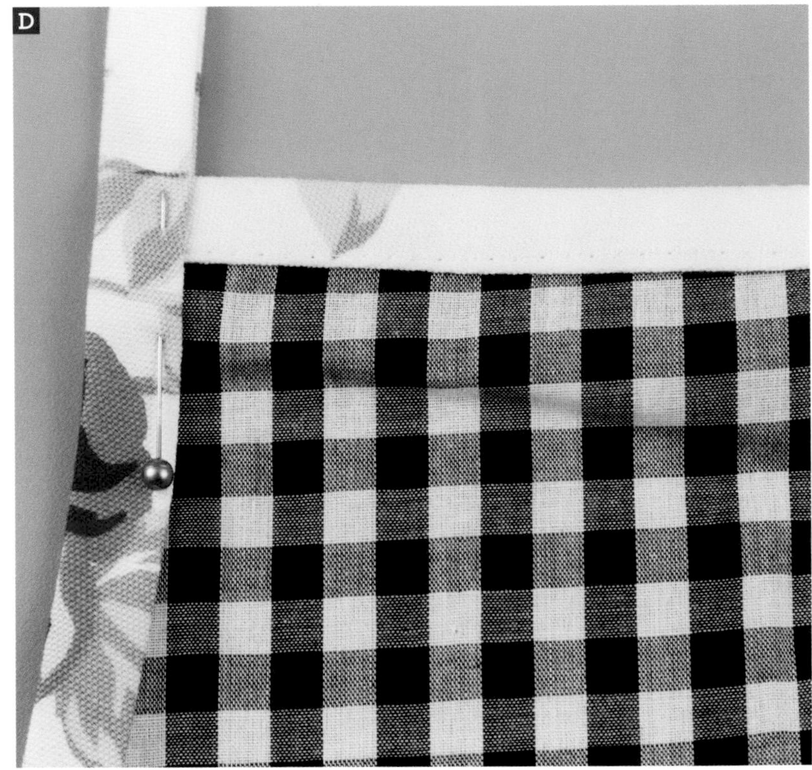

6 Starting at the end of one tie, sew the edges of the bias binding together. Continue sewing, catching the armhole fabric in the binding. Continue sewing the rest of the binding edges together until you get to the end of the other tie. Repeat on the other side of the apron (E).

7 Fold the ends of the ties over ¼"/6mm two times, and sew close to the fold (F).

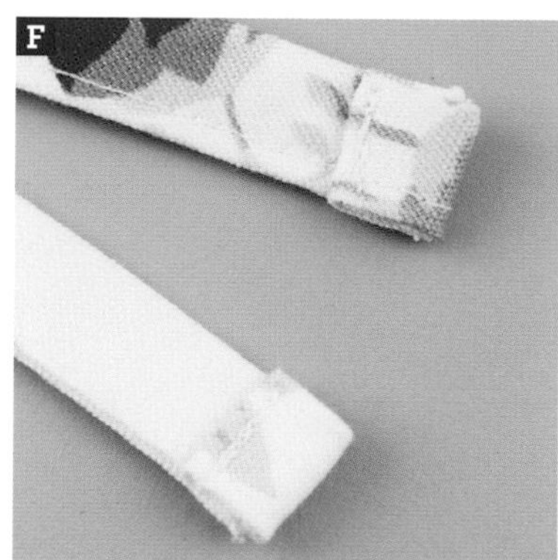

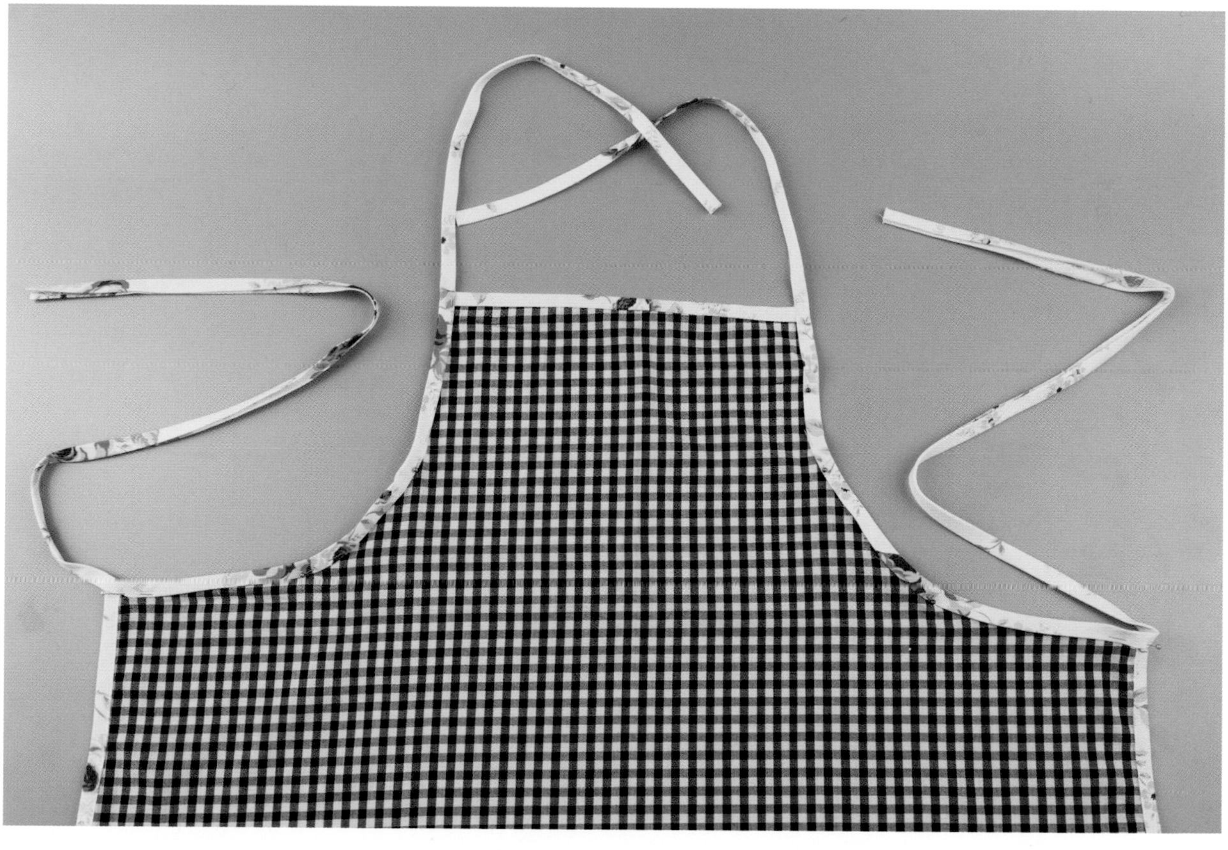

ENERG
(MALIN+

Spacious Spa Caddy

Designed by Christina Roy

LEVEL

This handy basket is perfect for so many things. Use it as a spa caddy, or for pens, stationery, washi tape, and all your other favorite writing or crafting supplies. It would also make a darling gift basket. Fill it with baby-themed items for a shower or with treats for the holidays.

FINISHED DIMENSIONS 7" × 7"/18cm × 18cm, not including the handles

SEAM ALLOWANCE Use ½"/13mm seam allowance unless otherwise noted

What You Need

FABRIC

Suggested fabrics include light- to medium-weight cotton and cotton blends.

- ½yd/45.5cm (or 2 fat quarters) of exterior fabric
- ½yd/45.5cm (or 2 fat quarters) of lining, handles, and binding fabric

ADDITIONAL SUPPLIES

- 1yd/91cm of light- to medium-weight fusible interfacing
- 1yd/91cm of fusible fleece

What You Do

CUT YOUR FABRIC

From the exterior fabric, cut:

- 1 bottom, 8" × 8"/20.5cm × 20.5cm
- 4 sides, 7" × 8"/18cm × 20.5cm
- 6 pockets, 5" × 8"/12.5cm × 20.5cm (see A on page 110)

From the lining, handles, and binding fabric, cut:

- 1 bottom, 8" × 8"/20.5cm × 20.5cm
- 4 sides, 7" × 8"/18cm × 20.5cm
- 2 handles 3" × 20"/7.5cm × 51cm
- 3 binding strips, 2" × 8"/5cm × 20.5cm
- 1 continuous binding strip, 2" × 33"/5cm × 84cm (piece this strip together if you're using fat quarters—see B on page 111)

From the interfacing, cut:

- 2 bottoms, 8" × 8"/20.5cm × 20.5cm
- 8 sides, 7" × 8"/18cm × 20.5cm
- 6 pockets, 5" × 8"/12.5cm × 20.5cm
- 2 handles, 3" × 20"/7.5cm × 51cm

From the fusible fleece, cut:

- 2 bottoms 7" × 7"/18cm × 18cm
- 8 sides 6" × 7"/15cm × 18cm

PREPARE THE SIDES AND HANDLES

1 Fuse the interfacing to the wrong side of all of the fabric and lining pieces, including the handles (not the binding strips).

2 Center and fuse the fusible fleece pieces to the bottom and sides of the exterior and lining fabrics, directly over the stabilizer from the previous step (A).

3 If you're using fat quarters, sew the binding pieces together with a ¼"/6mm seam allowance to make one 2" x 33"/5cm x 84cm-long binding strip.

A

4 Fold and press all the binding pieces, as directed in Pressing Bias and Straight Binding and Other Fabric Strips (page ix).

MAKE THE POCKETS

1 Pin two of the pockets with wrong sides together. Repeat with the other pocket pieces until you have three double-layer pocket pieces.

2 Unfold one edge of the 8"/20.5cm binding strips. Pin one binding strip to the long edge of each of the pocket pieces, right sides together and the unfolded edge aligned with the pocket edge, as shown. Stitch directly in the fold line (B).

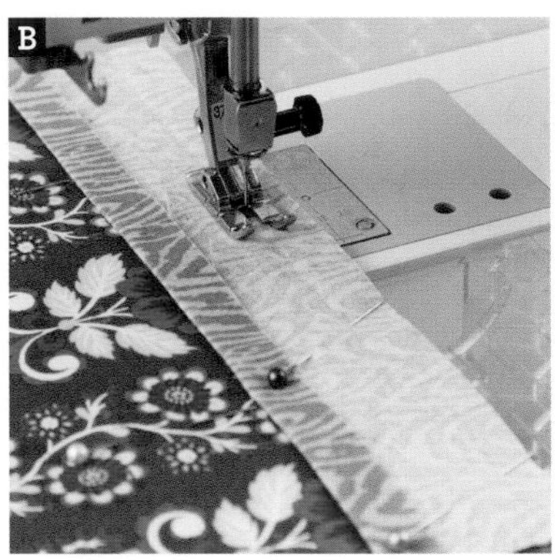
B

3 Flip the binding up and around the top of the pocket to encase the seam allowance. Press flat. Topstitch on the front of the binding, close to the lower edge (see Topstitching, page xii). Take care to catch the binding on the back of the pocket in the stitching. Repeat to bind the top edge of the other two pockets (C).

C

4 Pin one pocket piece to the right side of a side piece to make the pocket. The bottom edges should be even. Measure and mark six vertical lines on the pocket as shown on C on page 112.

5 Stitch along the vertical lines. Be sure to backstitch neatly at the top.

6 Pin the remaining two pocket pieces to two of the side pieces, aligning the bottom edges. Baste the pockets to the sides within the seam allowance (see Basting, page ix). There will be one side with no pocket (D).

D

ASSEMBLE THE EXTERIOR BASKET AND LINING

1 Lay out the exterior pieces as shown. The bottom edges of the side pieces will be sewn to the bottom piece with the right sides together (see D on page 113).

2 Pin one of the side pieces to the bottom piece, right sides together. Make sure to backstitch at all starting and stopping points.

3 Stitch the side to the bottom, starting and stopping ½"/13mm from each edge (this is important). If it helps, use the edge of the fusible fleece as a guide, since it is ½"/13mm from the side edges (E).

E

4 Pin and stitch the opposite side piece to the bottom. Be sure to start and stop stitching ½"/13mm from each edge. Press the seams open.

> TIP Make sure you press the seams open! It makes a huge difference in the finished product.

5 Pin and sew the remaining side pieces to the bottom. Again, be sure to start and stop stitching ½"/13mm from each edge. Press the seams open.

6 Fold up and pin two sides together. Stitch from the top edge to ½"/13mm from the bottom, so the side seam meets the bottom seam. Make sure to backstitch at all starting and stopping points.

7 Pin and sew the remaining sides together one at a time. You now have a nice little box. Trim the bottom corners and the seam allowances to a point toward the corners (F).

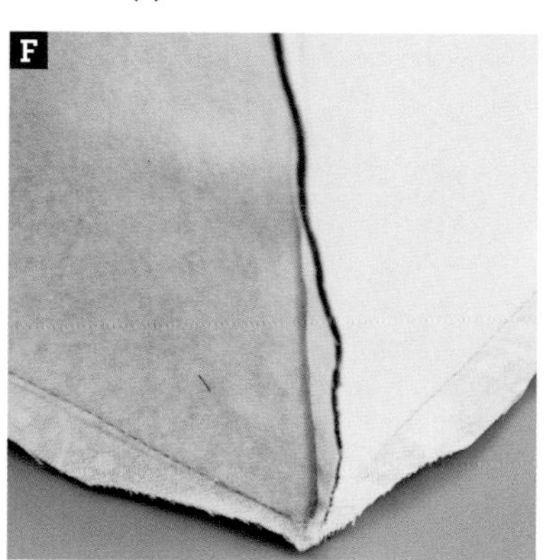

8 Turn the exterior basket right side out and press the edges, if needed, to give it shape.

9 Follow steps 1–8 to make the basket lining. Press the seams open.

> TIP Sew the lining pieces with a 5/8"/16mm seam allowance. This will make the lining fit better inside the basket.

ATTACH THE LINING

1 Place the lining inside the exterior basket, wrong sides together. Match up the side seams and pin around the top edge. Baste the top of the basket ¼"/6mm from the edge (see Basting, page ix). (G)

2 Unfold the remaining binding strip. Pin it around the top edge, leaving about 3"/7.5cm open and 3"/7.5cm-long tails free at both ends of the opening. Stitch the binding to the top of the basket directly in the uppermost fold line (H).

3 Pinch the binding to close the opening and pin them to mark the seam location, as shown. Make sure the binding fits the opening without buckling (I).

4 Stitch the binding ends together at the pin marking. There will be extra binding.

5 Trim away the extra binding and press the seam open. Finish sewing the binding to the top edge of the basket (J).

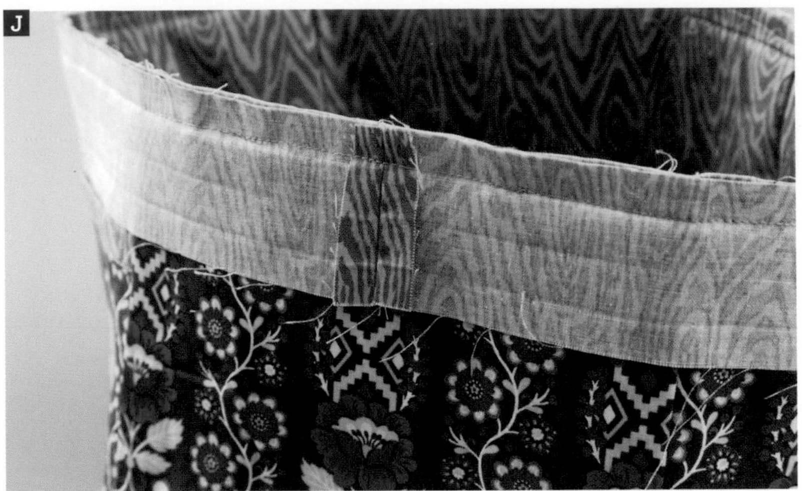
J

6 Flip the binding up and around the top of the basket. Press and refold the bottom edge of the binding. Pin the folded edge in place to encase the seam allowances and finish the top edge. Stitch along the folded edge of the binding.

SEW THE HANDLES

1 Fold the handle pieces lengthwise, right sides together. Pin and stitch along the long edge, leaving the short ends open.

2 Press the seams open. Turn the handles right side out through one end and press them flat with the seam running down the middle. This side, with the seam, becomes the wrong side.

3 Fold each handle end toward the right side, about 1½"/4cm, and pin it in place. Topstitch along both long edges of each handle (K).

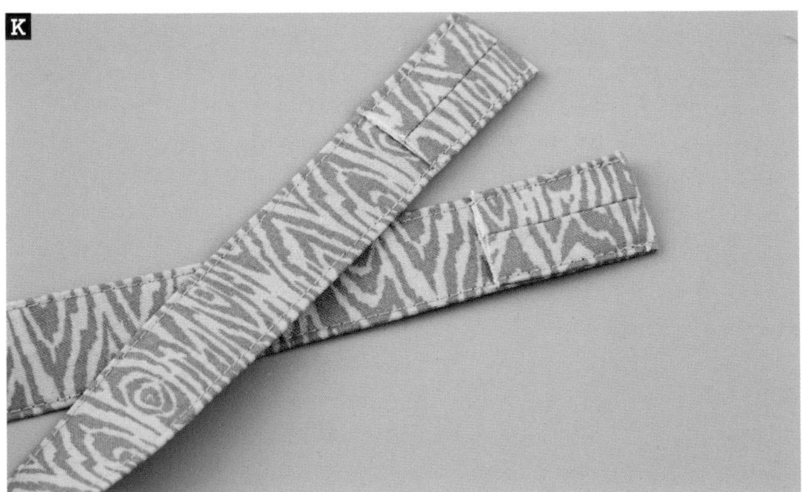
K

4 Pin the handles inside the basket 1"/2.5cm from the corner seams, with the folded ends against the basket lining so they will be hidden. Make sure the straps are not twisted.

5 Stitch the handles in place, as shown. Use the topstitching as a guide and stitch right on top of it where you can and then stitch an "X" in the middle to reinforce the handles (L).

L

6 Measure from the basket edge 3"/7.5cm up each side of both handles, and mark with a pin. Between pin markings, fold the handles in half so the edges meet, and pin (M).

M

7 Stitch the folded edges together, directly over the previous topstitching.

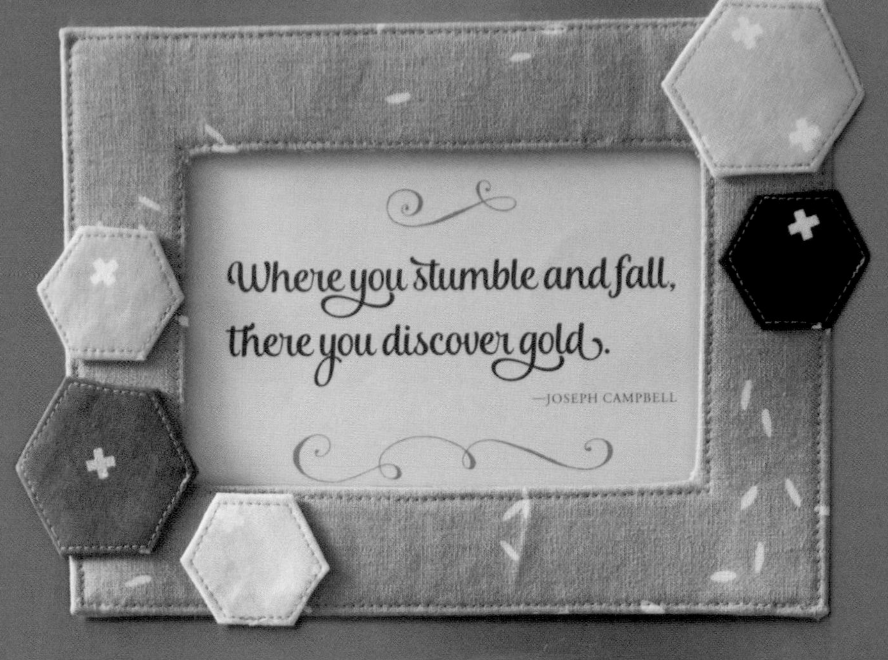
Where you stumble and fall,
there you discover gold.
—JOSEPH CAMPBELL

Photo Frame Fridge Magnet

SCRAP friendly!

Designed by Jenelle Clark

LEVEL

Decorate your fridge or your workspace with this handmade magnet frame. It's a great way to use up the last few scraps of your favorite fabric—and provide that boost of inspiration all of us need from time to time!

FINISHED SIZE Approximately 8" × 10"/20.5cm x 25.5cm, not including the hexi embellishments
SEAM ALLOWANCE No seam allowance required

What You Need

FABRIC

- A scrap of fabric at least 8" × 10"/20.5cm x 25.5cm cm for the frame.
- Coordinating fabric scraps for the hexi embellishments
- Template, page 114

ADDITIONAL SUPPLIES

- Cardstock
- Fusible extra-firm stabilizer
- Craft knife or scissors
- Magnetic canvas, 9" × 22"/ 23cm × 56cm
- Fabric marking pen
- Quick-drying fabric glue
- Pressing paper (optional)

What You Do

PREPARE THE TEMPLATE

1 Photocopy the hexi template (A on page 114) onto cardstock.

2 Cut out the template so you have two larger hexies and three smaller ones. Use the cardstock hexies as templates to cut the stabilizer and then use them to finish the backs of the fabric hexies.

CUT YOUR FABRIC

1 Using the cardstock hexi templates, trace the larger hexi two times and the smaller hexi three times onto the extra-firm fusible stabilizer.

2 Cut out five hexies.

From the fabric scraps, cut:
two squares 3" × 3"/7.5cm × 7.5cm and three squares 2½" × 2½"/6.5cm × 6.5cm for the hexies.

PREPARE THE FRAME

1 To prepare the frame, draw a 6" × 8"/15cm × 20.5cm rectangle on the fusible extra-firm stabilizer. Then draw an inside rectangle, 1¼"/3cm away from the outside rectangle. Carefully trim around both rectangles, using the craft knife or scissors.

2 Cut a 5½" × 7½"/15cm x 19cm rectangle from the magnetic canvas. On the back of this piece, draw an inside rectangle 1"/2.5cm away from all four edges. Carefully trim away the inside rectangle from the magnetic canvas, using the craft knife or scissors (A).

3 Cut an 8" × 10"/20.5cm × 25.5cm rectangle from the frame fabric. Then, use the fabric marking pen to mark the fabric as shown (see B on page 114).

4 Cut out the inside rectangle and carefully cut along each of the diagonal lines (B).

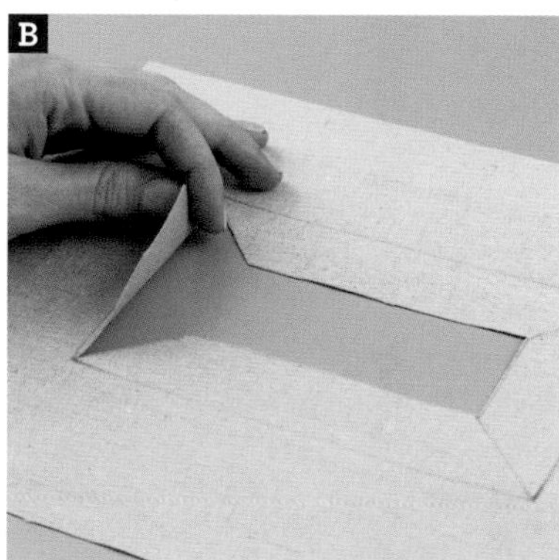

B

A

MAKE THE FRAME

1 Lay the prepared 8" × 10"/20.5cm × 25.5cm rectangle of fabric on your work surface, wrong side up. Place the stabilizer, fusible side down, on top of the fabric, centered over the rectangular markings (C).

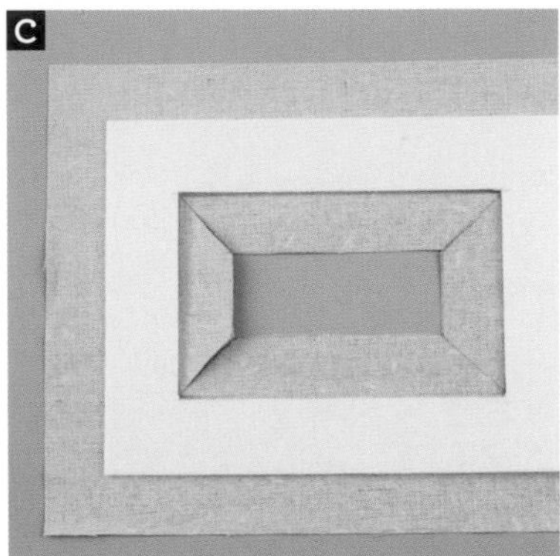

2 Carefully turn the fabric and stabilizer over and press to fuse the stabilizer and fabric together.

3 Apply a thin line of fabric glue on the wrong side, around the inside edge of the frame fabric. Then carefully fold back the four interior edges and adhere them to the stabilizer.

TIP As I folded and glued the fabric around the stabilizer, I found it helpful to place a sheet of pressing paper over my project and press each edge. This quickly sets the fold and dries the glue and the paper protects your iron from any extra glue.

4 Finish the outside edges of the frame by applying a small amount of glue directly on the stabilizer one side at a time. Carefully fold over the fabric edges to secure them to the stabilizer.

5 Topstitch around the interior and exterior edges of the frame (see Topstitching, page xiii), ⅛"/3mm from the edge (D).

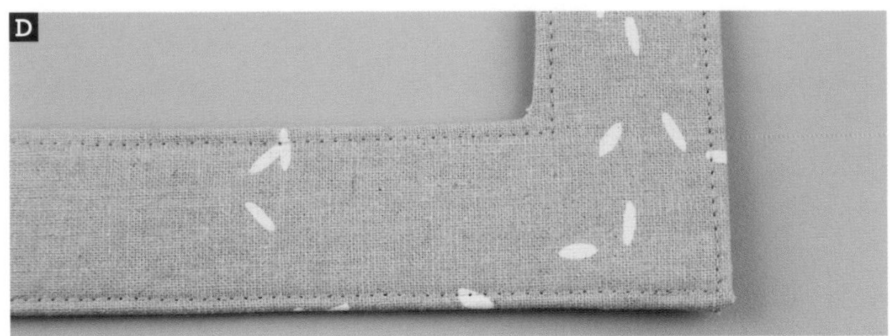

6 Apply glue to the back (white side) of the magnet frame. Use the interior edges of the frame to line up the magnet and secure it to the wrong side of the fabric-wrapped frame, sealing the unfinished edges of the fabric and covering the rest of the exposed stabilizer (E).

TIP Fold and glue the side edges first. Miter the corners and then fold and glue the long top and bottom edges.

MAKE THE HEXI EMBELLISHMENTS

1 Fuse one hexi, cut from stabilizer, to the wrong side of the center of each 2½"/6.5cm and 3"/7.5cm fabric square. Pair the larger fabric pieces with the larger hexies.

2 Trim the fabric around the stabilizer with the craft knife or scissors, leaving about ½"/13mm of fabric on each side (F).

3 Place a thin line of fabric glue along the top edge of the stabilizer. Fold over the fabric and adhere it to the stabilizer. Moving clockwise, apply glue and carefully fold over the fabric on each of the edges of the hexi, one at a time, mitering the corners and smoothing the fabric as you go. Press with pressing paper to protect your iron, if desired (see Tip on page 62). Repeat with each of the remaining hexies (G).

4 Topstitch around the front of each hexi ⅛"/3mm from the edge.

5 Apply glue to the back of each hexi cut from cardstock and secure them to the wrong side of each fabric hexi to cover the unfinished edges (H).

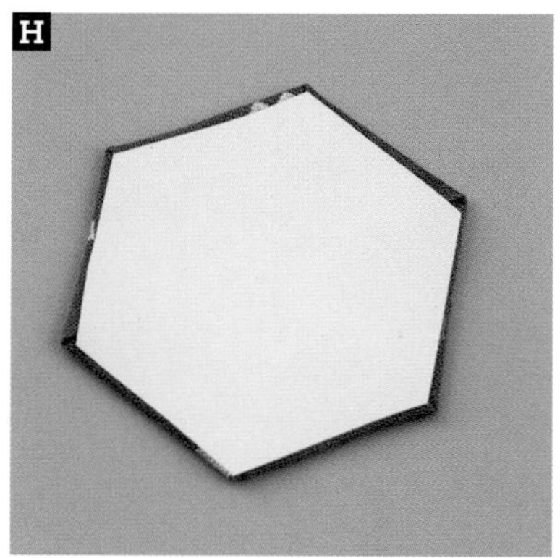

6 Arrange the hexies on the right side of the photo frame in your favorite configuration. Glue each hexi to the frame one at a time and allow to dry.

TIP You can create a custom frame for any of your favorite photos or postcards. You may even want to use your favorite image when considering how to lay out the hexies on the frame.

SCRAP friendly!

Cute Hexi Magnets

Designed by Jenelle Clark

SKILL LEVEL

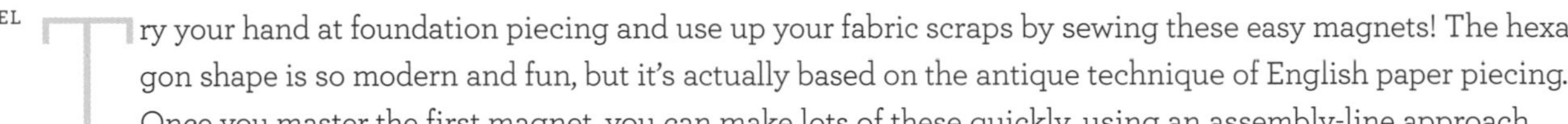
Try your hand at foundation piecing and use up your fabric scraps by sewing these easy magnets! The hexagon shape is so modern and fun, but it's actually based on the antique technique of English paper piecing. Once you master the first magnet, you can make lots of these quickly, using an assembly-line approach.

TIP After sewing these cute magnets, make the coordinating Photo Frame Fridge Magnet too (page 61).

FINISHED SIZE Approximately 2¾" x 3"/7cm x 7.5cm
SEAM ALLOWANCE Use ¼"/6mm seam allowance, unless otherwise noted

What You Need

FABRIC

- Coordinating fabric scraps (strips work best)
- ¼yd/23cm or less of thin muslin fabric
- Templates, page 115

ADDITIONAL SUPPLIES

- Cardstock
- Magnetic canvas
- Fusible extra-firm stabilizer
- Pressing paper (optional)
- Quick-drying fabric glue

What You Do

PREPARE THE TEMPLATE

1 Enlarge and photocopy hexi templates A and B on page 115 onto cardstock. Carefully trim around each hexi shape.

2 From the coordinating fabric scraps, cut an assortment of strips 5"/12.5cm long by various widths between ¾"/2cm and 1½"/4cm inches. Each hexi magnet will use five or six strips.

3 Trace the hexi template (A on page 115) three times onto the white side of the magnetic canvas and three times onto the fusible extra-firm stabilizer. Cut out the shapes.

4 Cut three 5"/12.5cm squares of thin muslin.

MAKE THE FOUNDATION PIECES

This project uses thin muslin fabric for the foundation and simple topstitching to secure the fabric scraps (see Topstitching, page xii).

1 Trace hexi template B three times onto the three pieces of thin muslin fabric.

2 Place a strip of fabric right side up on the center of the hexi shape. Refer to B on page 115 for suggested strip placement.

3 Place another fabric strip (any width) on top of the first fabric strip with the edges aligned and right sides together (A).

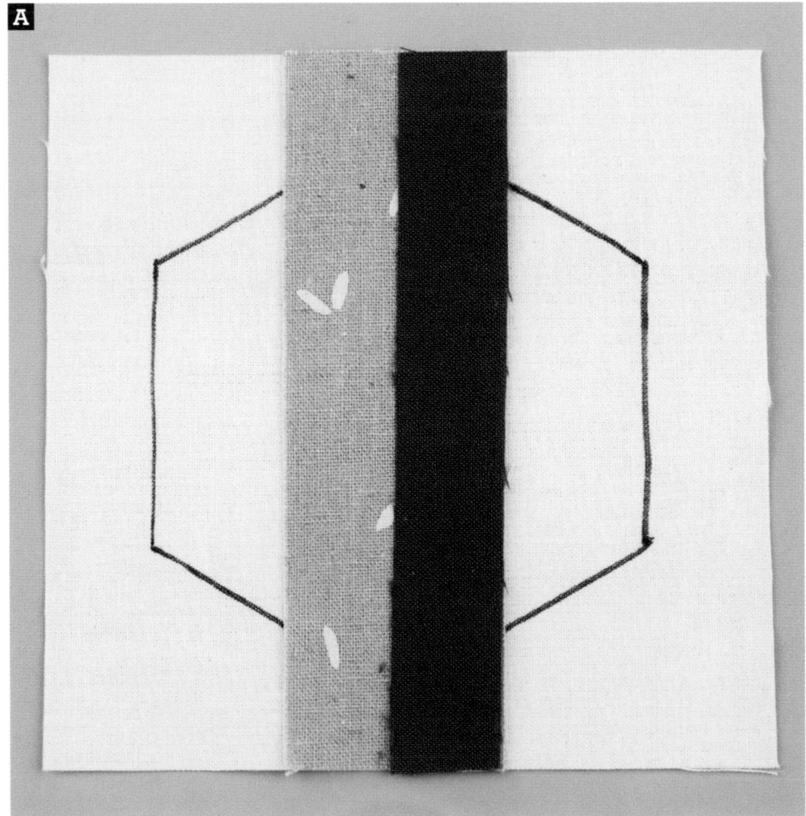
A

4 Sew the two fabric strips together through all layers. Open and press or finger-press the second strip away from the first. Topstitch on the second strip close to the seam (B).

5 Choose another fabric strip and align its edge with the unsewn edge of the first fabric strip. Once again sew this seam by sewing through all layers. Press or finger-press the strip away from the center and topstitch.

6 Continue adding strips until the entire hexi shape is covered.

TIP When sewing the final strips onto each side of the hexi shape, keep in mind that approximately ½"/13mm of fabric around the shape will be folded to the back of the magnet. Make sure to choose a wide enough strip (1"/2.5cm or bigger) for the sides to ensure that the fabric shows once the magnet is finished.

7 Use B on page 115 as a pattern to cut the hexagon shape from your foundation piece that has fabric strips sewn to it.

MAKE THE MAGNET

1 Center the fusible side of one of the extra-firm stabilizer hexi shapes against the wrong side of the fabric hexi so that there is ½"/13mm seam allowance all around (C).

2 Carefully turn the piece over and press to fuse the stabilizer and fabric together.

3 Place a thin line of fabric glue along one edge of the stabilizer. Fold over the edge of the fabric to adhere it to the stabilizer. Moving clockwise, apply glue, and carefully fold over the fabric on each of the edges, mitering the corners and smoothing the fabric as you go (D).

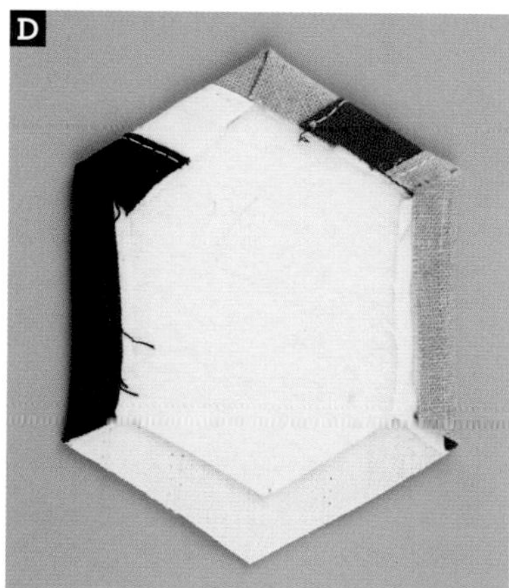

TIP If your fabric edges are resisting the glue, lay the piece right side down on your ironing board, cover with a piece of pressing paper (to protect your iron from the glue), and press the edges through the paper. This will quickly dry the glue and set the edges in place.

4 Topstitch around the hexi ⅛"/3mm from the edge (see Topstitching, page xii). (E)

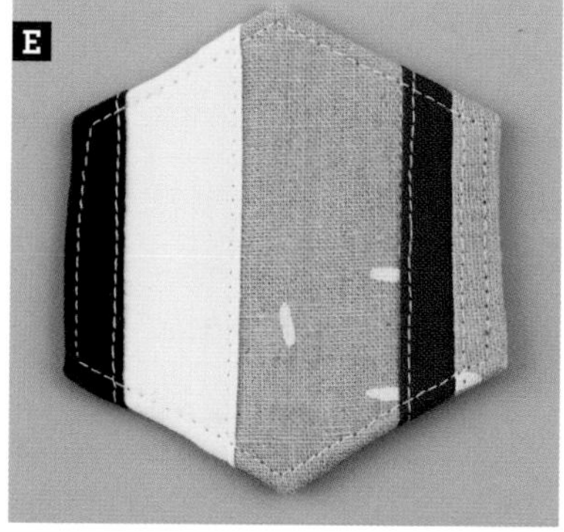

5 Apply fabric glue to the back (the white side) of one of the magnet shapes. Secure it to the wrong side of the hexi piece, sealing the unfinished edges of the fabric and covering the rest of the exposed stabilizer. Allow the glue to dry before using the magnet (F).

6 Repeat all of the steps to make two more magnets.

Festive "Buttoned-Up" Baskets

Designed by Jennifer Heynen, a.k.a. Jennifer Jangles

LEVEL

These stacking baskets are perfect for holiday décor because at the end of the year you can unbutton them, lay them all flat, and store them neatly away until you need them again. You can also use them for easy gift baskets . . . just fill with goodies and share!

FINISHED SIZES

- *Small:* 3" tall × 4" wide/7.5cm × 10cm
- *Medium:* 3½" tall × 5½" wide/9cm × 14cm
- *Large:* 4" tall × 7½" wide/10cm × 19cm

SEAM ALLOWANCE Use ¼"/6mm seam allowance, unless otherwise noted

What You Need

FABRIC

For the medium and large baskets:

- ½yd/45.5cm (or 1 fat quarter) of cotton fabric for the exterior
- ½yd/45.5cm (or 1 fat quarter) of cotton fabric for the lining

For the small basket:

- ⅓yd/30.5cm (or 1 fat quarter) cotton fabric for the exterior
- ⅓yd/30.5cm (or 1 fat quarter) cotton fabric for the lining
- Template, page 116

ADDITIONAL SUPPLIES FOR EACH BASKET

- ½yd/45.5cm heavyweight sew-in interfacing (⅓yd/30.5cm for the small basket)
- 12"/30.5cm oval cord elastic or ⅛"/3mm-wide elastic
- Chopstick or turning tool (optional)
- 4 matching buttons, approximately 1"/2.5cm in diameter
- 6"/15cm square of green wool felt for the holly leaves

What You Do

CUT YOUR FABRIC

For the large basket, cut:

- 15" × 15"/38cm × 38cm squares, one each from the exterior fabric, lining fabric, and heavyweight interfacing
- Stack the three squares and cut a 33/4" × 33/4"/9.5cm × 9.5cm square from each corner of the three layers. The piece should look like a plus sign.

For the medium basket, cut:

- 12" × 12"/30.5cm × 30.5cm squares, one each from the exterior fabric, lining fabric, and heavyweight interfacing
- Stack the three squares and cut a 3¼" × 3¼"/8cm × 8cm square from each corner of the three layers. The piece should look like a plus sign.

For the small basket, cut:

- 9" × 9"/23cm × 23cm squares, one each from the exterior fabric, lining fabric, and heavyweight interfacing
- Stack the three squares and cut a 2½" × 2½"/6.5cm × 6.5cm square from each corner of the three layers. The piece should look like a plus sign.

For each basket, use the holly template on page 116 to cut four holly pieces from the green wool felt.

SEW THE BASKETS

1 Trim ¼"/6mm from the top edge of the heavyweight interfacing piece. This edge will be the "open edge" for turning.

2 Place the two fabric pieces with the right sides together. Lay the interfacing on top and pin the three layers together. All the sides will align except for the top open edge.

3 Measure 1"/2.5cm down from the raw edge on the top left side of the plus sign and mark with a pin. This is where the elastic loop will go. Rotate the plus sign and mark three more elastic locations on the three remaining sides. Be sure to mark on the left side each time (A).

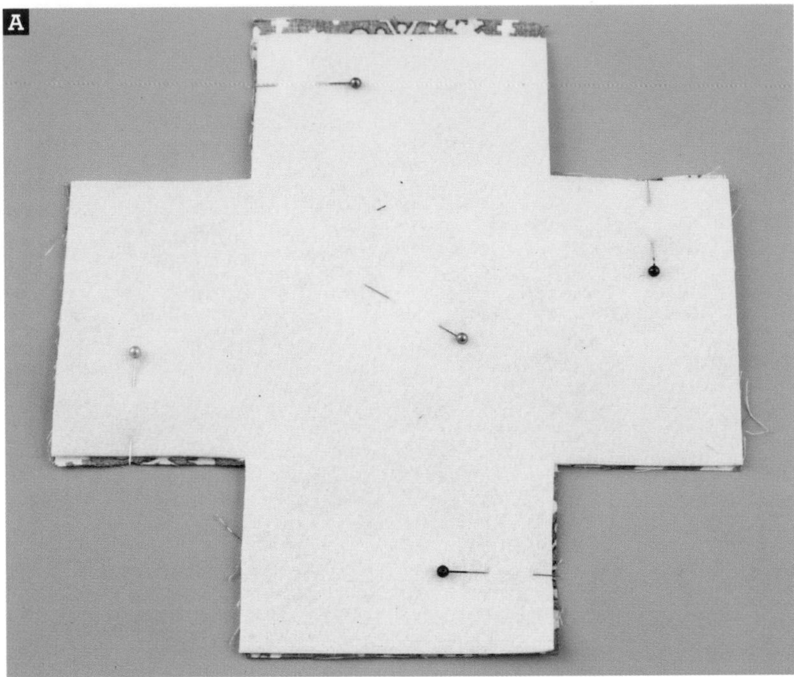

4 Cut four pieces of cord or ⅛"/3mm-wide elastic, each one 3"/7.5cm long.

5 Sew around all the outer edges, beginning on one side of the top edge and finishing on the opposite side of the top edge. Do not sew across the top edge. Pivot at the corners and insert a piece of elastic, folded in half, at each pin marking. Make sure the loop faces the inside, that the ends of the elastic are caught in the stitching, and that the loop is long enough to go around your buttons (B).

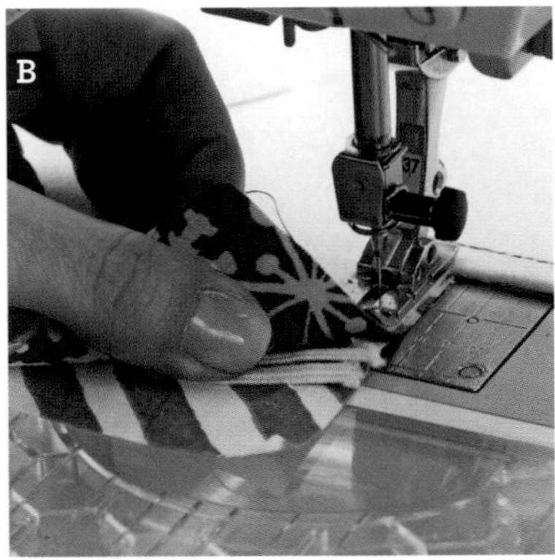

6 Trim across the outer corners, clip to the stitching at each inner corner, and trim the seam allowances to ⅛"/3mm (C).

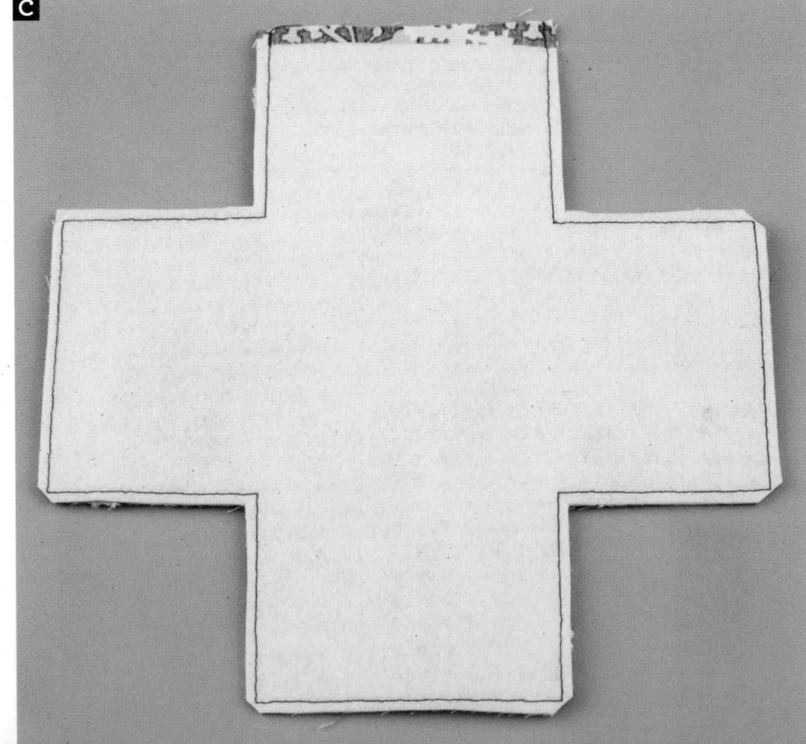

7 Turn the basket right side out, using the chopstick or turning tool (if needed) to push out all of the corners. Press the wrinkles out of the basket piece. Press the raw edges at the opening to the inside. Hand-stitch the opening closed (D).

8 Fold the sides of the basket up. Stack a button on top of the end of a holly leaf and sew a button/holly leaf to each side, opposite the elastic loop (E).

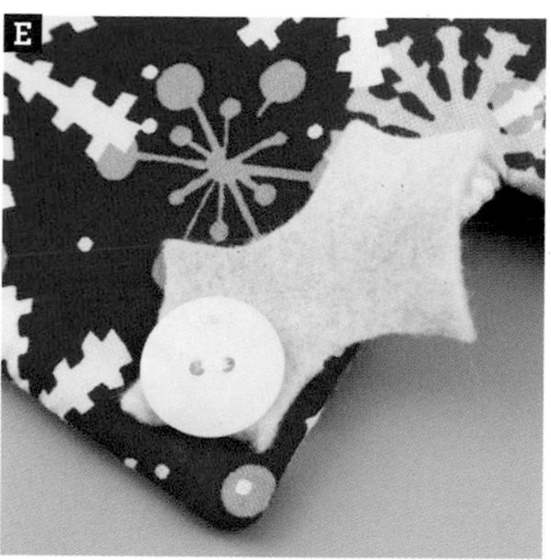

9 Button up the sides of the basket to finish.

123456
#lovetosew

SEWING FOR THE LITTLE ONES

It's one of my favorite things to do: sew for my children. I'm sure you feel the same, and it's likely your kids will get as much joy out of using these adorable projects as you will making them.

Kiddie Backpack

Designed by Caroline Fairbanks-Critchfield

L LEVEL

Perfect for a preschooler, this small backpack is just the right size for a snack and a toy. The side button tabs cinch it in, but they can be left unbuttoned for more space inside. There is a small, handy front pocket under the flap.

FINISHED SIZE Approximately 8" long × 8" wide × 4" deep/20.5cm × 20.5cm × 10 cm at the base, not including the straps

SEAM ALLOWANCE Use ⅜"/10mm seam allowance, unless otherwise noted

What You Need

FABRIC

Suggested fabrics include light- to medium-weight wovens, such as quilting cotton, cotton/linen blends, and home décor fabrics.

- ½yd/45.5cm of fabric for the exterior
- ½yd/45.5cm of fabric for the lining
- ½yd/45.5cm of fabric for the flap and straps
- Small pieces of fabric for the pocket, hanging loop, and button tabs

ADDITIONAL SUPPLIES

- 1yd/91cm of fusible fleece interfacing
- 3 buttons, ¾"–1"/2–2.5cm in diameter
- Fabric marking pen
- Old CD or small bowl

You can make a grown-up version with a more sophisticated pattern or solid fabric and 24"/61cm-long straps.

What You Do

CUT YOUR FABRIC

From the exterior fabric, cut:

- 1 front exterior, 11" × 13"/28cm × 33cm
- 1 back exterior, 11" × 13"/28cm × 33cm

From the lining fabric, cut:

- 1 front lining, 11" × 13"/28cm × 33cm
- 1 back lining, 11" × 13"/28cm × 33cm
- 1 flap, 9" × 10"/23cm × 25.5cm

From the fabric, cut:

- 1 flap, 9" × 10"/23cm × 25.5cm
- 2 straps, 6" × 18"/15cm × 45.5cm

From the small pieces of pocket, hanging loop, and button tabs fabric, cut:

- 1 pocket, 9" × 7"/23cm × 18cm
- 2 button tabs, 4" × 3½"/10cm × 9cm
- 1 hanging loop, 2" × 5"/5cm × 12.5cm

From the fusible fleece interfacing, cut:

- 2 front/back pieces, 11" × 13"/28cm × 33cm
- 1 flap, 9" × 10"/23cm × 25.5cm
- 2 strips, 1½" × 18"/4cm × 45.5cm

PREPARE THE PIECES

1 Fuse the front and back pieces of fusible fleece interfacing to the wrong side of the front and back pieces cut from the exterior fabric. Fuse the smaller piece of fusible fleece to the wrong side of the flap cut from the coordinating fabric (not the lining piece).

2 Fold and press the hanging loop and the straps like bias tape (see Pressing Bias and Straight Binding and Other Fabric Strips, page ix).

3 Place the narrow strips of fusible fleece interfacing inside the folded straps, refold, and press (A).

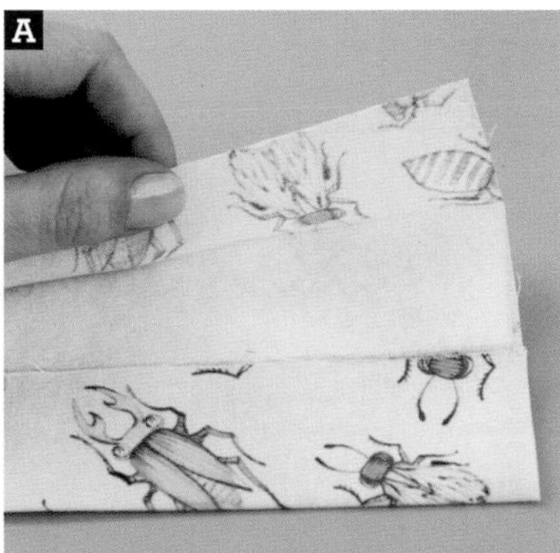
A

4 Topstitch along the long edges of the small hanging loop and the straps (see Topstitching, page xii). Topstitch one more time down the center of each strap (B).

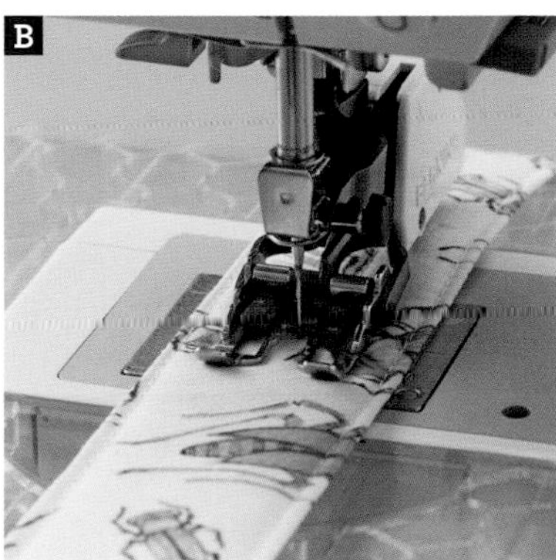
B

TIP Topstitching straps is easier with a walking foot, if you have one.

5 Fold the button tab pieces in half, with the shorter edges right sides together. Stitch along one short edge and one long edge. Trim the corners.

6 Turn the tabs right side out and fold the raw edges ⅜"/10mm to the inside. Press flat. Sew a buttonhole (to fit your buttons) near the sewn ends of the tabs (C).

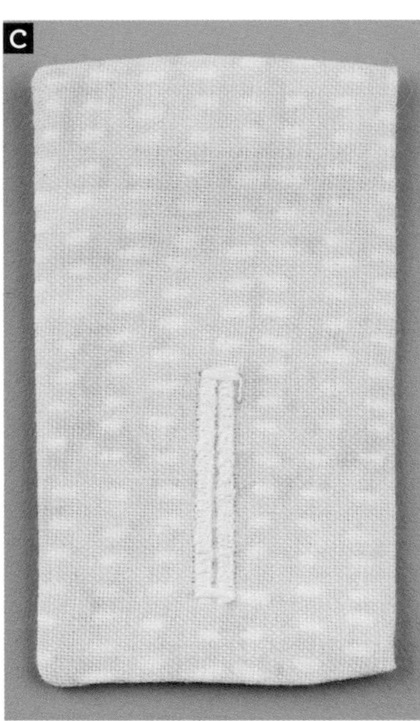

C

MAKE THE BACKPACK FRONT

1 Fold the front pocket in half, with the shorter edges right sides together. Pin and stitch around three sides, leaving a 3"/7.5cm opening for turning.

2 Trim the corners and turn the pocket right side out. Press. Topstitch (see Topstitching, page xiii) close to the folded edge (to make the top of the pocket). Press the edges of the opening ⅜"/10mm to the inside. Sew one of the buttons to the center of the pocket.

3 Center and pin the pocket to the front exterior piece, 3½"/9cm above the bottom edge. Stitch the pocket in place along the bottom and side edges (closing the opening at the same time). Set the backpack front piece aside (D).

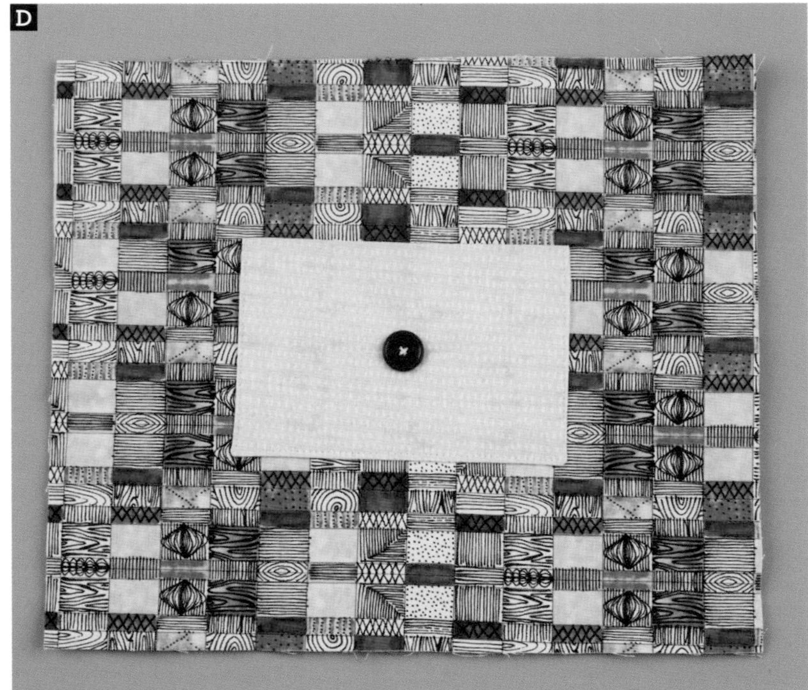

D

MAKE THE BACKPACK BACK

1 Pin the button tabs to the back exterior piece with the stitched end of the tabs lined up with the side edges and the top edge of the tabs 1½"/4cm below the top edge of the back exterior piece.

2 Stitch the tabs in place along the pressed (open) ends, closing the openings at the same time.

3 Fold the back in half to find and mark the center at the top edge. Fold the hanging loop in half and pin both raw edges to the top on either side of the center mark.

4 Pin the top edges of the straps on either side of the hanging loop. Sew along the top, ¼"/6mm from the edge, to secure the straps and the hanging loop.

5 Pin the opposite ends of the straps to the sides of the exterior piece, 3"/7.5cm above the bottom edge (make sure they aren't twisted). Sew them in place ¼"/6mm from the edge (E).

E

SEW THE BACKPACK TOGETHER

1 Pin the button tabs back, away from the side edges so they are not caught in the side seams. Pin the two backpack exterior pieces, with the right sides together, around the side and bottom edges, being careful not to catch the button tabs, hanging loop, and straps in the seam (F).

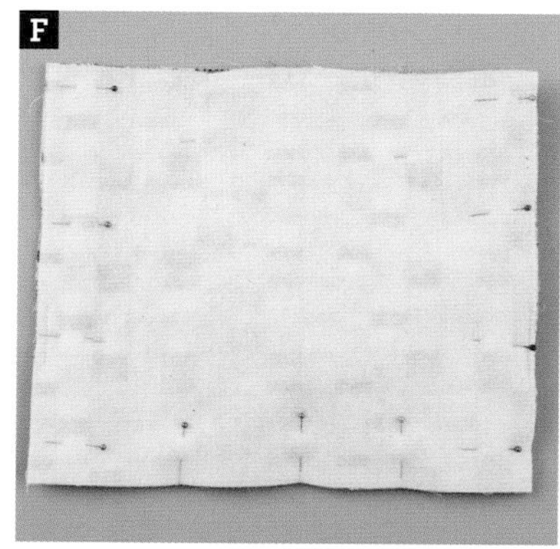
F

2 Stitch around the sides and the bottom of the backpack exterior. Press the seams open.

3 Box both corners as follows: Flatten a corner against the bottom of the bag, centering the bottom seam. Draw a line 4"/10cm long across the corner and pin (G).

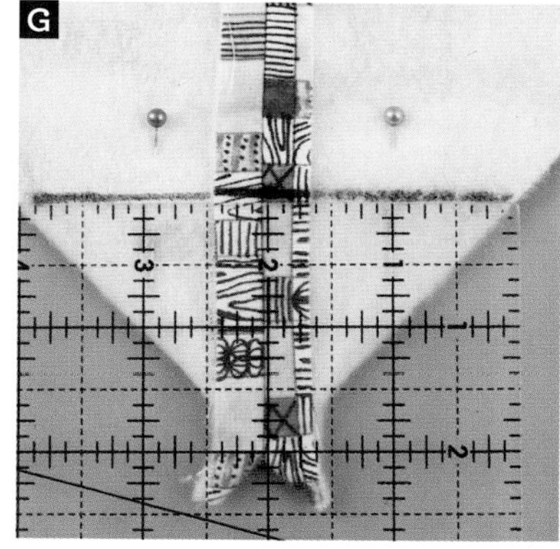
G

4 Stitch across the marked line. Trim away the corner, leaving ⅜"/10mm seam allowance (H).

5 Pin and stitch the lining pieces, right sides together, around the side and bottom edges, leaving a 5"/12.5cm opening for turning on the bottom edge. Press the seam allowances open. Box the corners the same way as for the exterior.

6 With the backpack exterior turned right side out, slide the lining over the exterior so right sides are together and side seams are aligned. Pin and stitch all around the top edge (I).

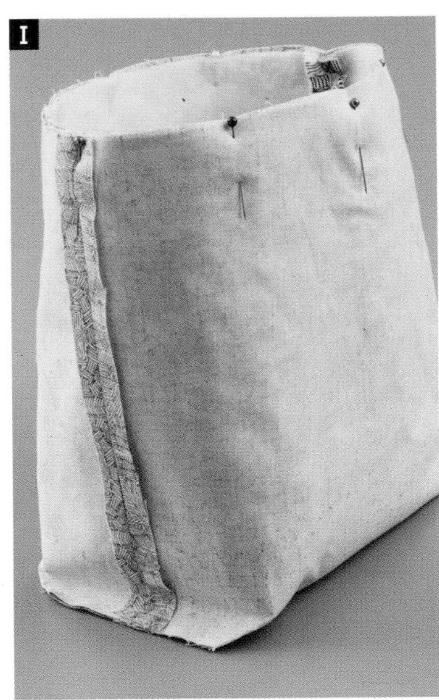

7 Turn the backpack right side out through the opening in the lining. Turn the raw edges at the opening ⅜"/10mm to the inside and press. Sew the opening closed.

8 Gently press the lining to the inside of the backpack around the top edge. Topstitch all the way around ⅛"/3mm from the edge (see Topstitching, page xiii). (J)

MAKE THE FLAP

1 Place the two flap pieces with right sides together and the 10"/25.5cm-long edges at the top and bottom. Use an old CD or a small bowl to mark curved edges around the bottom corners. Trim away the corners along the markings (K).

2 Pin and stitch around the whole flap, leaving a 4"/10cm opening for turning along the top straight edge. Trim the seam allowance at the corners and cut notches (see Clipping and Notching, page x) into the curved edges. (L)

3 Turn the flap right side out through the opening. Press the flap, turning the raw edges ⅜"/10mm to the inside. Topstitch all the way around the flap, close to the edges (see Topstitching, page xii).

4 Fold the flap in half to find the center. Draw a vertical line for a buttonhole starting 1"/2.5cm above the bottom edge. Sew the buttonhole (M).

FINISH

1 Pin the straight edge of the flap to the back of the backpack, overlapping the edges by ¼"–⅜"/6–10mm, as shown (N).

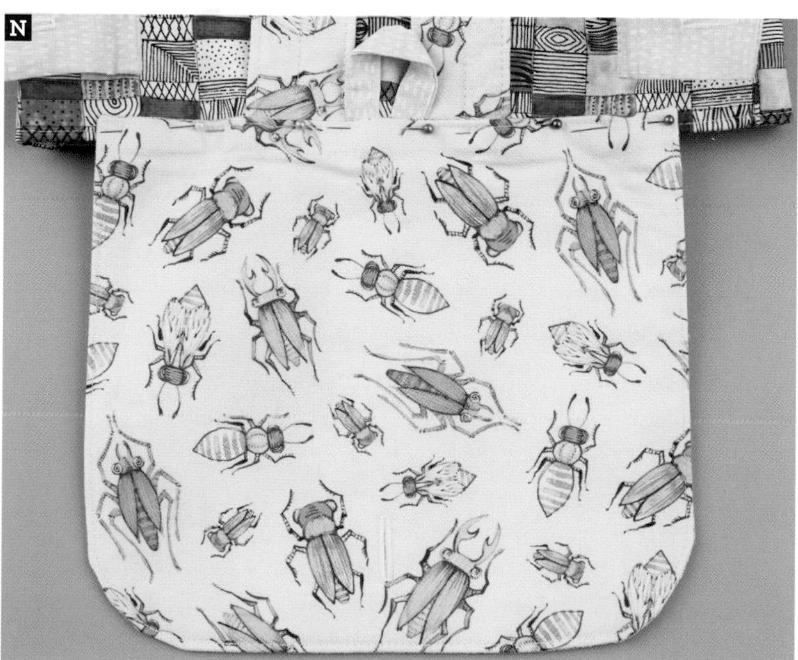

2 Attach the flap by stitching over the topstitching already on the straight edge of the flap.

3 Hand-sew the two remaining buttons to the front of the backpack, each 1½"/4cm away from the side seams and even with the buttonholes on the tabs (O).

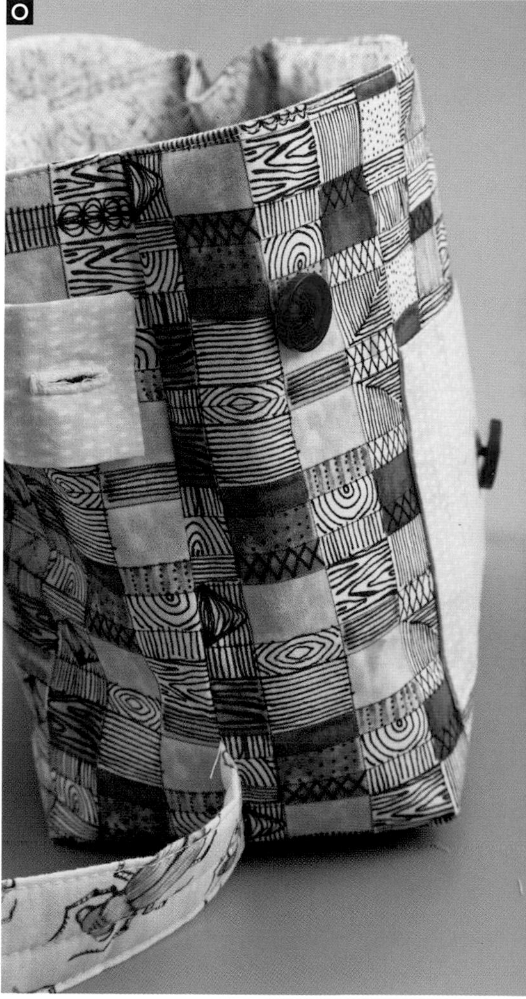

Easy Wallet with Pockets

SCRAP friendly!

Designed by Caroline Fairbanks-Critchfield

LEVEL

This sweet bifold wallet is fun and practical. Inside there is a pocket for bills and two small pockets that close to securely hold coins and other treasures. Customizing the wallet is easy, too. For example, you can leave off the hook-and-loop tape on the coin pockets to make card slots, or divide the bill pocket with stitching down the middle to make two smaller pockets.

FINISHED SIZE Approximately 4" × 5"/10cm x 12.5cm, closed
SEAM ALLOWANCE Use a ⅜"/10mm seam allowance, unless otherwise noted

What You Need

FABRIC

Suggested fabrics include light- to medium-weight wovens, such as quilting cotton.

- 6" × 10"/15cm × 25.5cm piece of fabric for the exterior
- 6" × 10"/15cm × 25.5cm piece of fabric for the lining
- 5½" × 31"/14cm × 79cm strip of fabric for the inside pockets

ADDITIONAL SUPPLIES

- 6" × 20"/15cm × 51cm piece of medium-weight fusible woven interfacing
- 9"/23cm length of hook-and-loop tape (both sides)
- Chopstick or other turning tool
- Fabric marking pen or chalk

What You Do

CUT AND FUSE FABRIC

1 Cut your fabric pieces to the sizes specified. Cut the fusible interfacing into two 6" × 10"/15cm × 25.5cm pieces.
2 Fuse the interfacing to the 6" x 10"/15cm x 25.5cm interior and exterior wallet pieces.
3 Cut the hook-and-loop tape into two sets, one set 4¾"/12cm long and the other set 4¼"/11cm long.

MAKE THE WALLET

1 Pin the 6" × 10"/15cm × 25.5cm interior and exterior wallet pieces with the right sides together. Stitch around the edges (as shown with dotted line, below), leaving a 3"/7.5cm opening at one short end for turning. Trim the corners diagonally (A).

2 Turn the wallet right side out and use the chopstick or turning tool to push the corners out fully, if needed. Press flat, turning the raw edges at the opening to the inside.

3 Pin and stitch the softer (loop) side of the 4¾"/12cm-long hook-and-loop tape to the lining side of the wallet, close to the short end with the opening. This will stitch the opening closed at the same time (B).

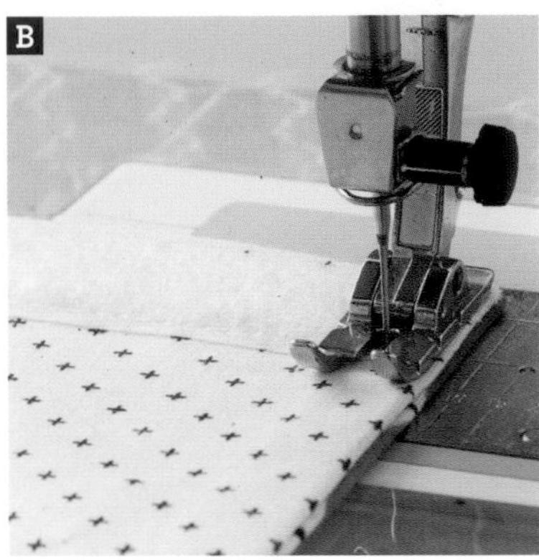
B

4 Turn the wallet over and sew the remaining piece of the 4¾"/12cm long hook-and-loop tape to the opposite end of the wallet on the exterior side (C).

MAKE THE POCKETS

1 Fold the 5½" × 31"/14cm × 79cm strip of fabric in half with the short ends and right sides together. Stitch around the three open sides (as shown with dotted lines, below), leaving a 3"/7.5cm opening at the short end for turning. Be sure to backstitch on either side of the opening. Trim the corners diagonally (D).

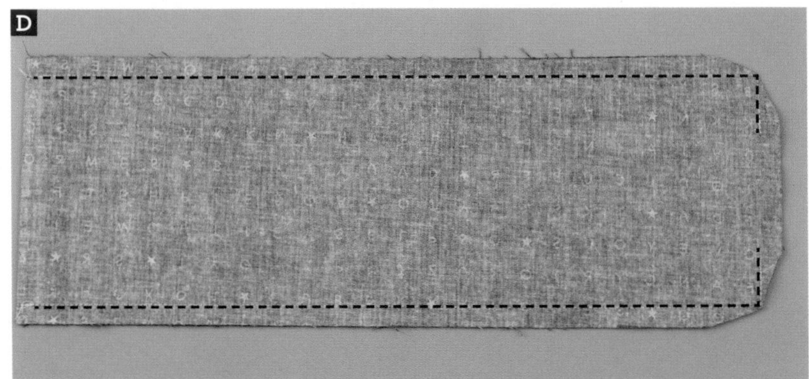
D

2 Turn the pocket piece right side out and use the chopstick or turning tool to push the corners out fully, if needed. Press flat, turning the raw edges at the opening to the inside.

3 Cut the remaining set of hook-and-loop tape in half vertically to make two long, narrow sets. Sew the softer (loop) side of each set along the ends of the pocket piece on the same side. This will stitch the opening closed at the same time.

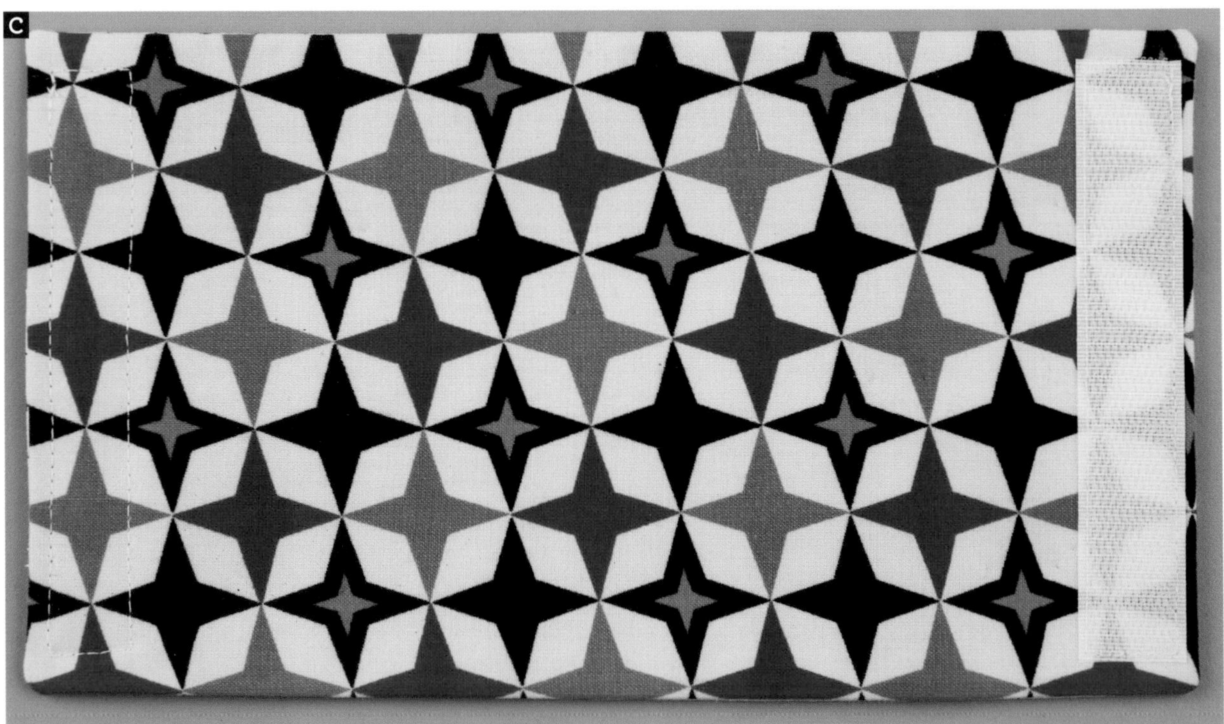
C

4 Fold the pocket piece in half to find the center. Use your chalk or fabric marker to draw a line down the center. Pin and stitch the remaining hook-and-loop strips to the pocket piece ⅜"/10mm away from each side of the center line. The strips should be ¾"/2cm apart (E).

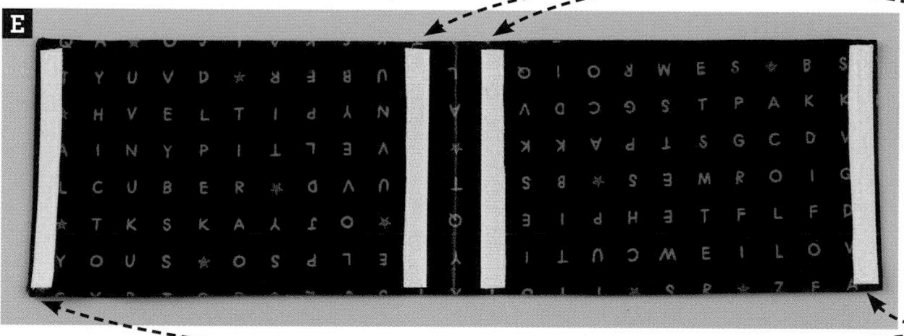

5 Fold the outer edges of the wallet so the corresponding pieces of the hook-and-loop tape meet to make the two small pockets. Topstitch ⅛"/3mm from the top edge (see Topstitching, page xii), backstitching neatly at the beginning and end.

SEW THE WALLET AND POCKETS TOGETHER

1 Pin the pocket piece to the interior side of the wallet with the bottom and left edges of the wallet and pocket piece aligned and the soft hook-and-loop strip on the right side (F).

2 Sew the pocket to the inside of the wallet along the side and bottom edges of the pocket piece, ⅛"/3mm from the edge (G).

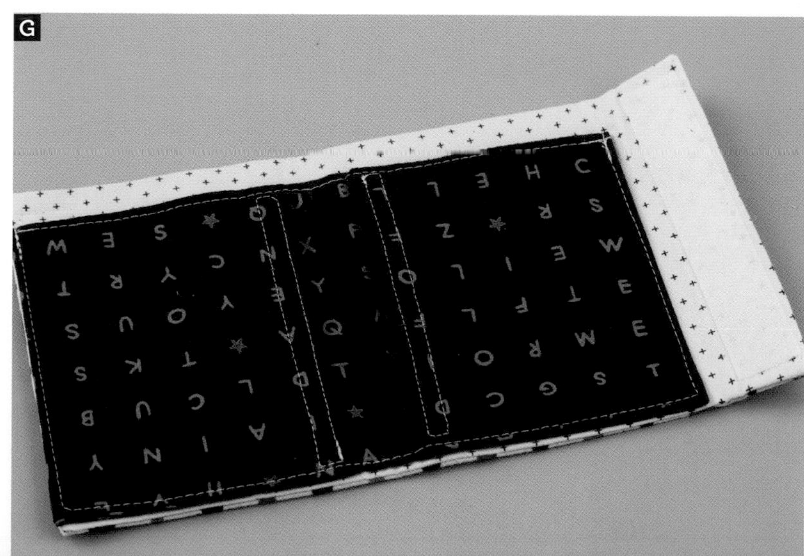

SCRAP friendly!

Felt and Fabric Hair Baubles

Designed by An Kuppens

LEVEL

Plastic hair baubles, move over! These felt and fabric baubles are soft and comfy against the head, and cuter to boot. They use only a tiny bit of fabric and are quick to make in five easy steps. Sew a whole bunch for your favorite little girl!

FINISHED SIZE Each bauble is approximately 1"/2.5cm in diameter, not including the hair elastic
SEAM ALLOWANCE No seam allowance required for this project

What You Need

FABRIC

- Scraps of lightweight fabric, 3"/7.5cm square or larger
- Template, page 117

ADDITIONAL SUPPLIES

- 1"/2.5cm felted wool balls (available at craft stores)
- Hair elastics

What You Do

1 Using the 3"/7.5cm-diameter circle template on page 117, cut two circles for each hair elastic.

TIP Our 3"/7.5cm circle template works great with 1"/2.5cm felted wool balls. If you want to try using a different-size ball, measure around the circumference of the ball and cut a circle with the same diameter as the ball circumference.

TIP This project is very easy to hand-sew. Simply sew step 2 by hand with long stitches, and then continue as directed.

2 Set your sewing machine to the longest stitch length. Sew around each circle about ⅛"/3mm away from the edge. Do not backstitch. Leave long tails of thread (A).

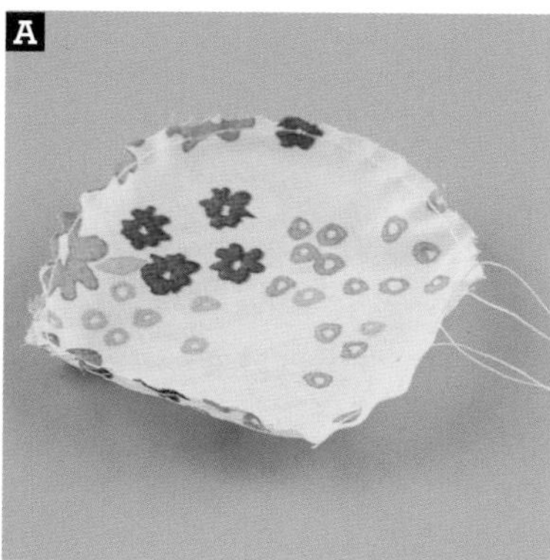
A

3 Place a felt ball in the center of one fabric circle and pull the tails of thread to close the fabric around the ball. Tie a secure knot with the thread ends (B).

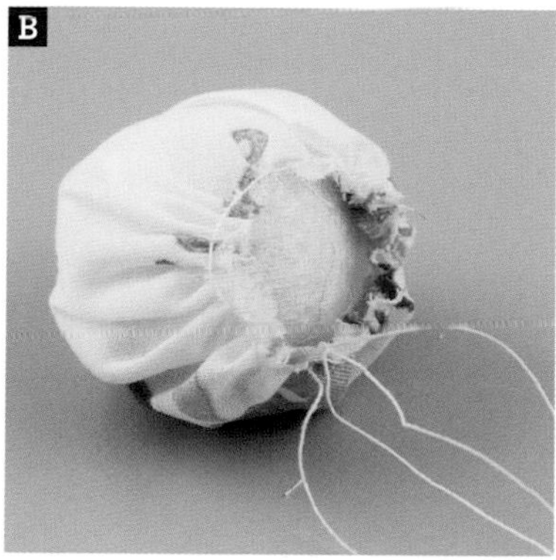
B

4 Insert one of the tails of thread into a needle, and make 8–10 stitches by hand to pull the fabric even tighter around the ball. Knot again to secure the fabric (C).

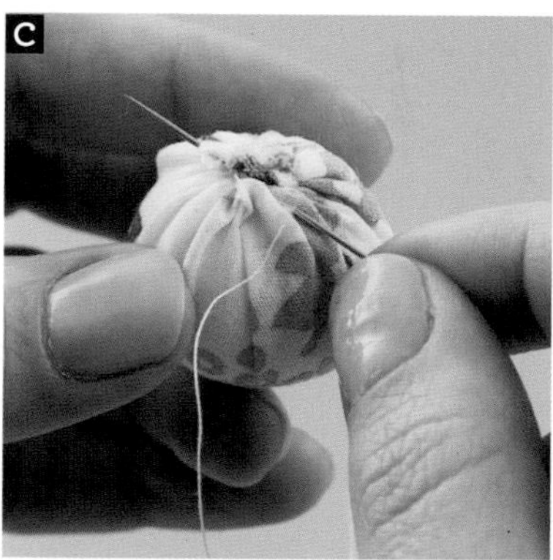
C

5 Repeat steps 3 and 4 to make a second ball. Hand-sew both balls to a hair elastic (D).

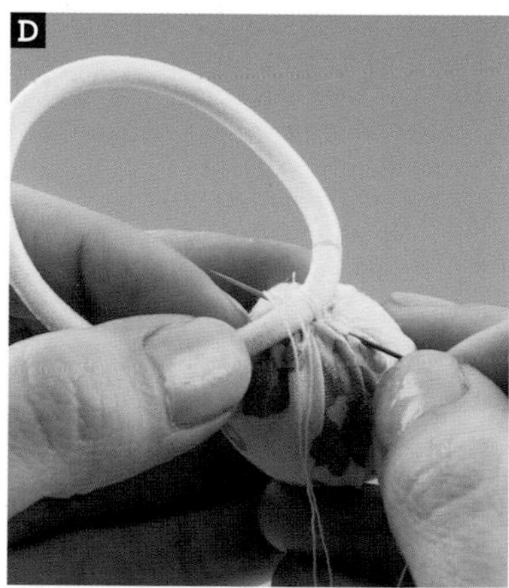
D

SCRAP friendly!

Color-Block Headband

Designed by An Kuppens

LEVEL

Sew a strip of your favorite fabric scraps together to make this cute headband. Make a variety, in girls' sizes, as well as teens'/women's sizes. You can even skip the color blocking and make super-easy headbands from a single fabric.

FINISHED SIZES The teens'/women's headband is approximately 21"/53.5cm in diameter and the girls' headband is approximately 19"/48.5cm in diameter

SEAM ALLOWANCE Use ⅜"/10mm seam allowance, unless otherwise noted

Note: When the dimensions differ for a teens'/women's headband in the instructions, the amount will be shown in parentheses.

What You Need

FABRIC

- Scraps of colorful print and solid fabrics, approximately 3" × 2"/7.5cm × 5cm to 3" × 8"/7.5cm × 20.5cm
- ⅛yd/11.5cm of fabric for the lining
- Fabric scrap, at least 3½" × 7"/9cm × 18cm for the elastic casing
- Templates, page 118

ADDITIONAL SUPPLIES

- 3"/7.5cm length of elastic, ¼"/6mm wide
- Chopstick or other turning tool
- Tweezers

What You Do

CUT YOUR FABRIC

From the fabric for the lining, cut:

- 1 girls' or teens'/women's headband (A and B on page 118)
- 2 girls' or teens'/women's elastic casings (A and B on page 118)

From the elastic, cut:

- 1 piece 2⅜"/6cm for a girls' headband (C on page 118) or
- 1 piece 2¾"/7cm for a teens'/women's headband (D on page 118)

MAKE THE HEADBAND

1 Stitch the fabric scraps together to make a strip at least 3"/7.5cm wide and 18"/45.5cm (20"/51cm) long. Press the seam allowances toward the darker pieces (A).

2 Cut one headband (A and B on page 118) from the pieced strip of fabric.

3 Pin one elastic casing piece to one end of the headband with right sides together and stitch. Press the seam allowance open.

TIP To make two pieces of fabric join at an angle, lay one piece on top of the other, both right sides up. Use a ruler to mark and cut the desired angle. Then flip the top piece over and stitch the pieces together.

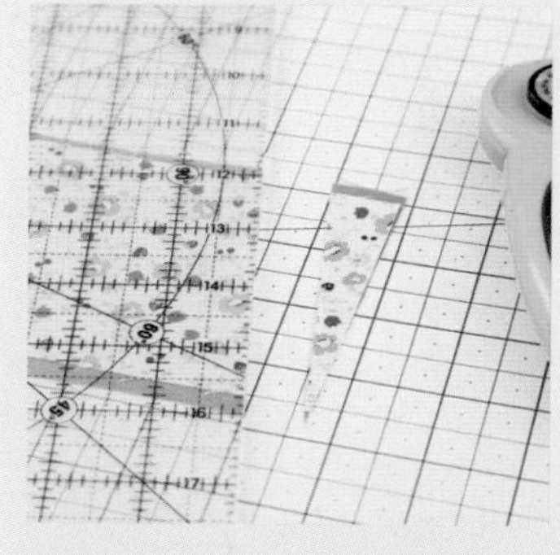

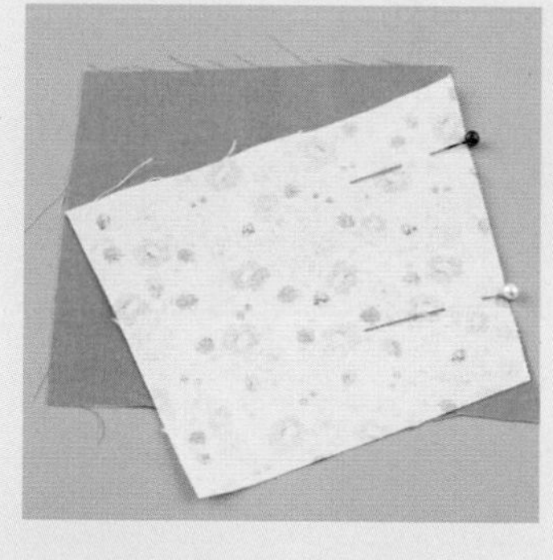

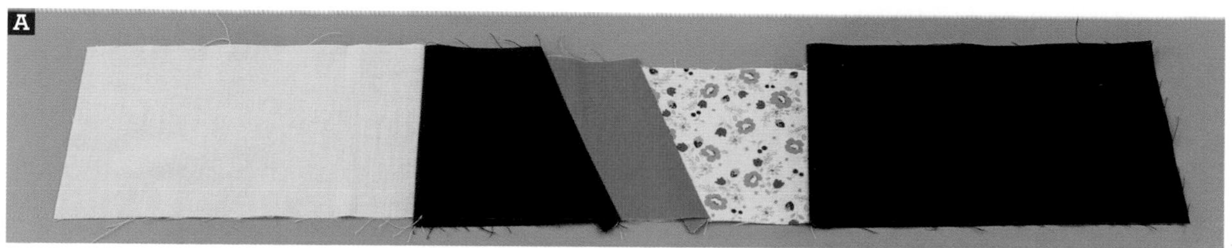

4 Repeat for the headband lining piece and the remaining elastic casing piece, adding the length of elastic on top, as shown. Stitch back and forth over the elastic so it is attached securely. Press the seam allowance toward the headband (B).

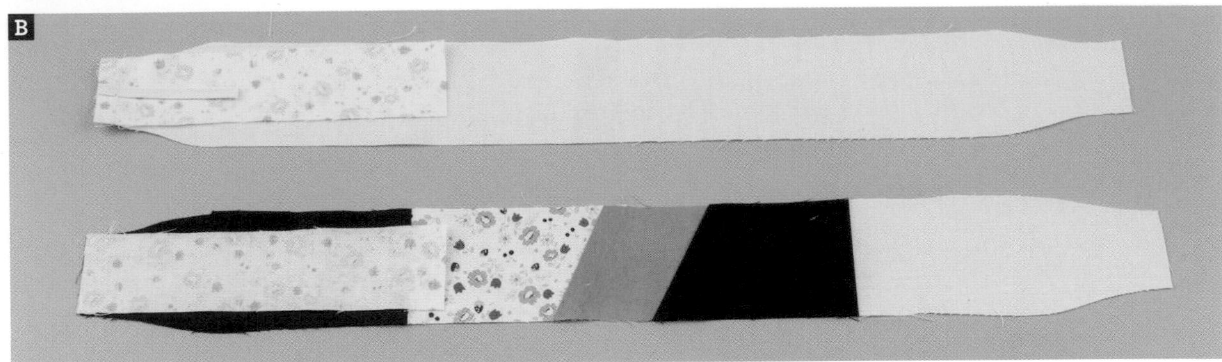

B

5 Pin the headband and lining pieces, right sides together, and stitch along both long edges (C).

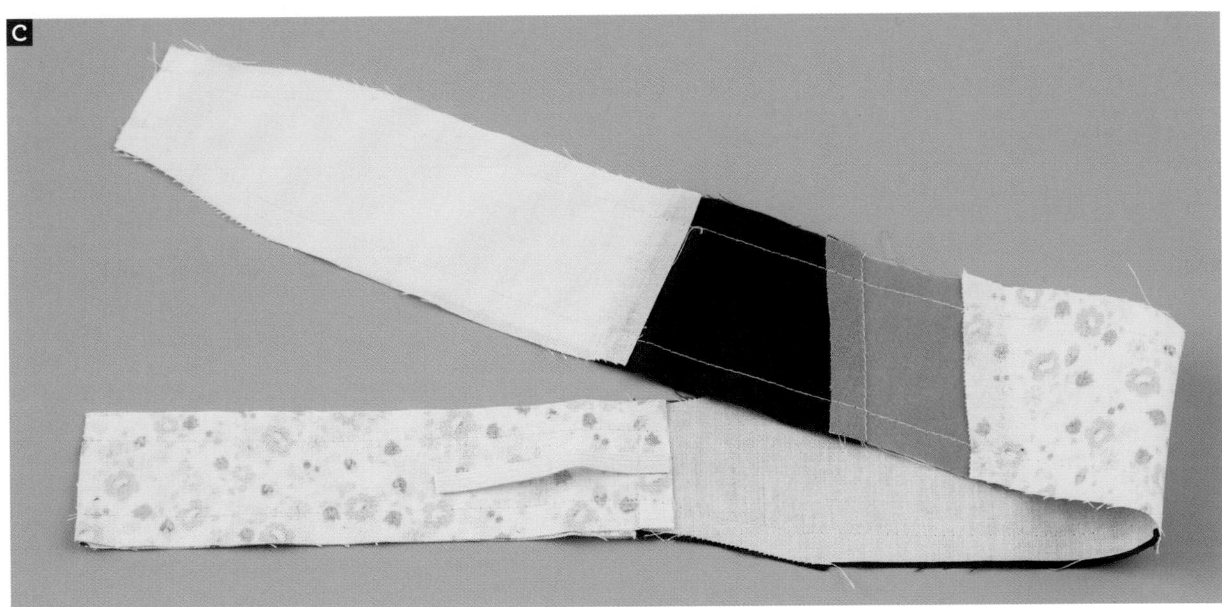

C

6 Turn the headband right side out, using the chopstick or turning tool (see Tip).

TIP Baste one of the short edges closed (see Basting, page ix). Use the chopstick or turning tool to push the end that is basted through the headband, turning the headband right side out.

7 Remove the basting stitches from the previous step, if you used them, and press the headband with your iron.

8 Catch the end of the piece of elastic with the tweezers. Pull it out a bit, and align the end of the elastic just beyond the edge of the fabric. Make sure the elastic is not twisted. Pin it in place, and secure it by stitching back and forth about ¼"/6mm from the edge (D).

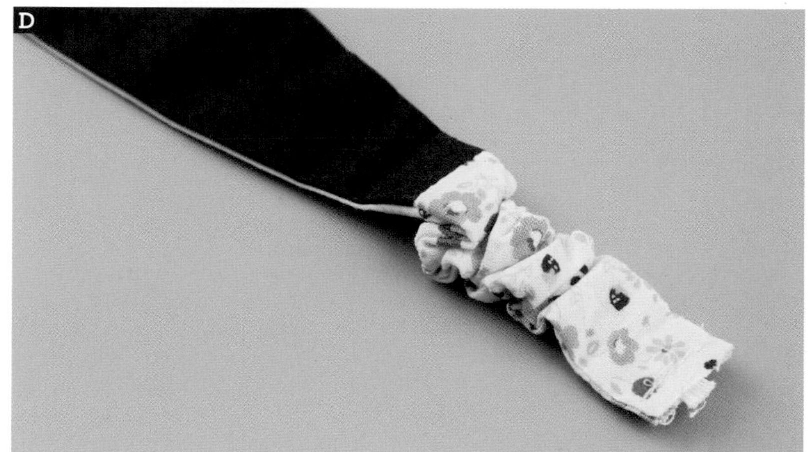
D

TIP If you have trouble inserting the elasticized end into the headband end, cut about ½"/13mm off the headband end. Press the ends to the inside again, and now it will be big enough to fit the elasticized end.

9 On the other end of the headband, fold the raw edges of the opening to the inside about ⅜"/10mm. Press.

10 Slide the elasticized end into the open end so that there is an overlap of about ⅜"/10mm. Make sure the headband is not twisted. Topstitch across the folded end (see Topstitching, page xii) to close the headband and secure the elastic (E).

E

Lunch-in-a-Snap Tote

Designed by Virginia Lindsay

LEVEL ● ●

Your kids will love healthy lunches in this fun lunch tote. The handle on this boxy little bag unsnaps on either side so it's easy to pivot out of the way. Insulated batting helps keep food hot or cold so you may want one for yourself, too!

FINISHED SIZE Approximately 8" × 6" × 4"/20.5cm × 15cm × 10cm, not including the handle
SEAM ALLOWANCE Use ⅜"/10mm seam allowance, unless otherwise noted

What You Need

FABRIC

- ½yd/45.5cm of light- to medium-weight cotton fabric for the exterior, such as quilt-weight cotton or cotton canvas
- ½yd/45.5cm of lightweight cotton fabric for the lining, such as quilt-weight cotton
- Template, page 119

ADDITIONAL SUPPLIES

- 1½ yd/137cm of medium-weight fusible interfacing
- ½yd/45.5cm of insulated batting
- 2 size 16 snap closures and the required snap setter for your brand of snaps
- 1 zipper, 12"/30.5cm or longer
- Zipper foot
- Chopstick or turning tool
- Double-sided sewing adhesive (see Fabric and Notions Sources, page 123)
- Fabric marking pen

What You Do

CUT YOUR FABRIC

From the exterior fabric, cut:
- 1 body, 11" × 24½"/28cm × 62cm
- 2 side panels, 4" × 8"/10cm × 20.5cm
- 1 handle, 6" × 18"/15cm × 45.5cm

From the lining fabric, cut:
- 1 body, 11" × 24½"/28cm × 62cm

From the fusible interfacing, cut:
- 1 body, 11" × 24½"/28cm × 62cm
- 2 side panels, 4" × 8"/10cm × 20.5cm
- 1 strap, 6" × 18"/15cm × 45.5cm

From the insulated batting, cut:
- 1 body, 11" × 24½"/28cm × 62cm

PREPARE YOUR FABRIC

1 Fuse the interfacing to the wrong side of all the exterior fabric pieces, according to the product instructions.

2 Refer to the pattern template (A on page 119). Mark the shape of the body template on the exterior fabric, lining, and insulated batting pieces. Cut out the three pieces.

MAKE THE HANDLE

1 Fold the short ends of the handle piece ¼"/6mm to the wrong side and press.

2 Press the handle piece as directed in Pressing Bias and Straight Binding and Other Fabric Strips (page ix).

3 Topstitch ⅛"/3mm away from all four edges (see Topstitching, page xii).

INSTALL THE SNAPS

1 Affix one side of the snaps to each end of the handle, ½"/13mm from the end. Follow the product instructions to attach the snap correctly. Set the handle aside (A).

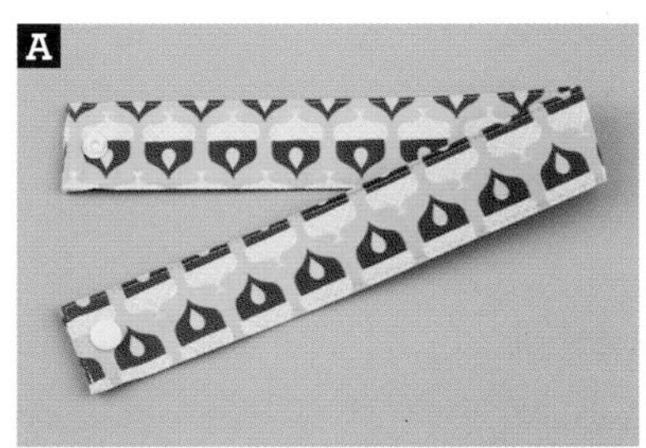

A

2 Install the opposite sides of the snaps. Transfer the markings for the snap locations from the pattern template onto the exterior body. Attach the snaps following the product instructions.

MAKE THE SIDE PANELS

1 Fold the side panels in half lengthwise so they measure 2" by 8"/5cm × 20.5cm.

2 Topstitch across the folded edge of both pieces (see Topstitching, page xii). Set aside (B).

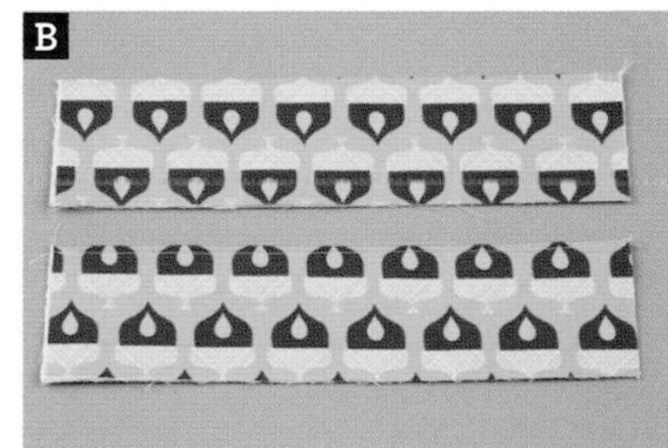

B

ATTACH THE ZIPPER

1 Install the zipper foot. Center the zipper over one side of the exterior body piece, right sides together, as shown. Stitch with a ¼"/6mm seam allowance (C).

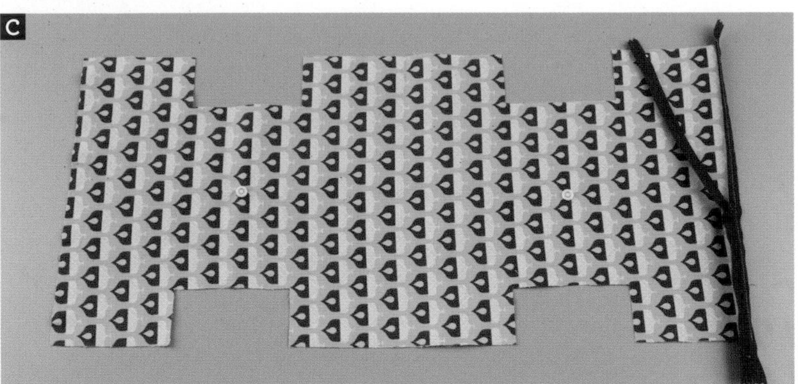

2 Fold the exterior in half and pin the other zipper tape to the opposite side, right sides together. Make sure all the edges line up. Stitch with a ¼"/6mm seam allowance (D).

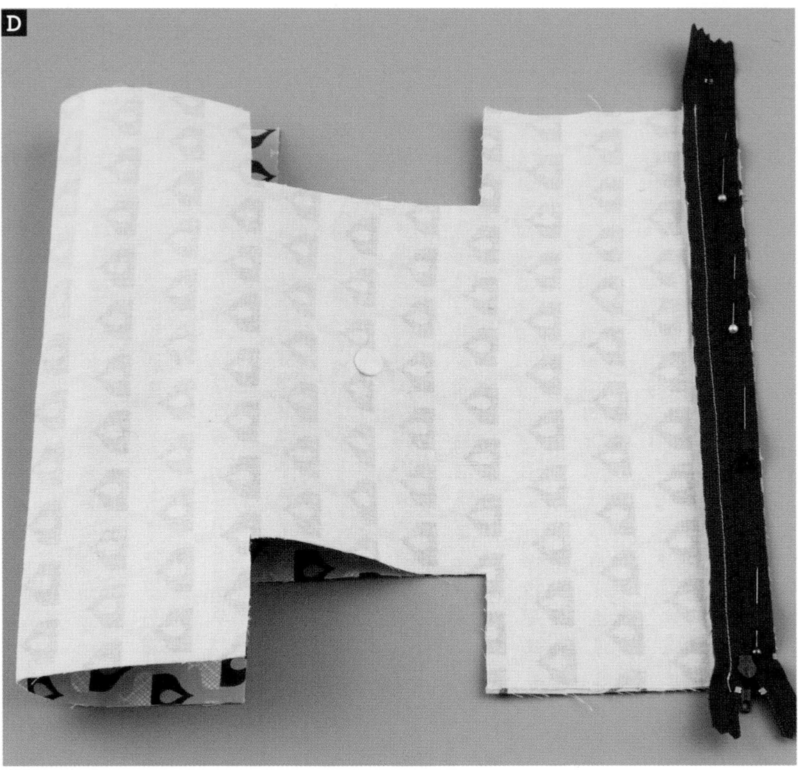

3 With the tote inside out and the zipper closed, center the zipper over what will become the bottom of the tote. Sandwich the side panels between the sides of the tote with the folded, topstitched edges facing toward the center and the raw edges aligned. Pin in place (E).

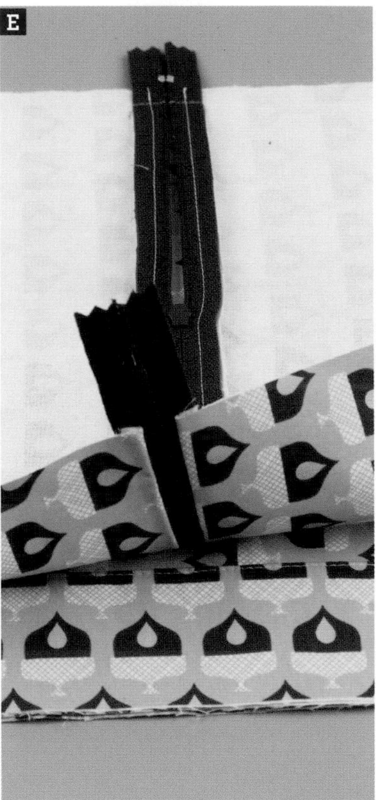

4 With the zipper tapes pinned in place at the side panels, open the zipper halfway. Add extra pins, if needed, to secure the zipper. Stitch across both sides. Trim away the zipper ends.

MAKE THE CORNERS

1 To make the corners and turn the exterior into a box, pinch together the cut-out corners so the zipper is centered and the edges line up, as shown (F).

F

2 Make sure that the side panels are folded toward the side with the zipper. Pin and sew across each corner.

3 Turn the exterior right side out through the zipper opening. Poke out the corners with the turning tool. Set aside.

MAKE THE INSULATED-BATTING LINING

1 Position the insulated batting over the wrong side of the lining body piece with the insulated side down. Baste along the sides (the shorter ends), ⅜"/10mm from the edge (see Basting, page ix).

2 Press the lining ⅜"/10mm toward the wrong side along the basting line. Repeat on the other side (G).

G

3 Fold the lining sides toward the middle, as shown. The edges should not meet; instead leave a center gap of about ¼"/6mm. Pin in place (H).

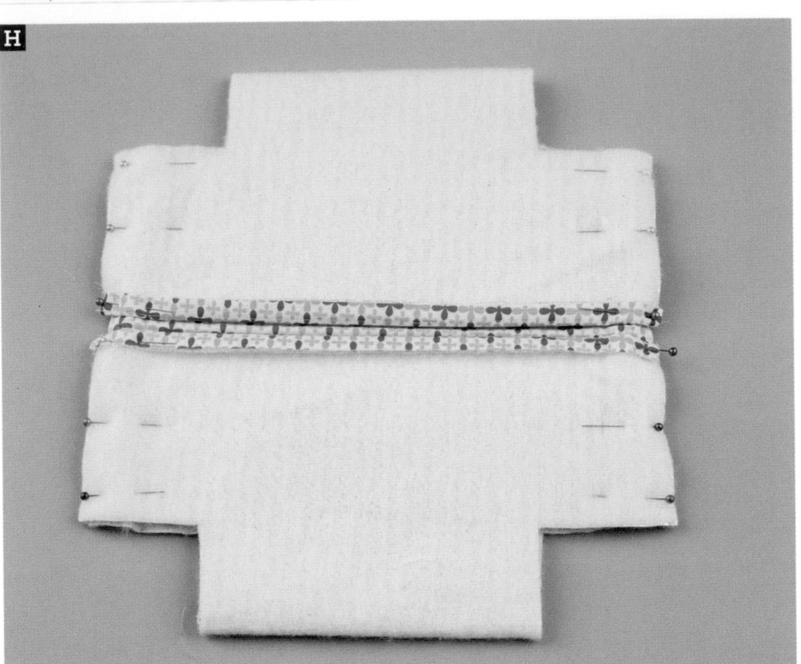

4 Stitch the sides together, right over the ¼"/6mm gap.

5 Apply strips of double-sided sewing adhesive to the folded edges of the lining. This will make attaching the lining to the exterior easier in the next step (I).

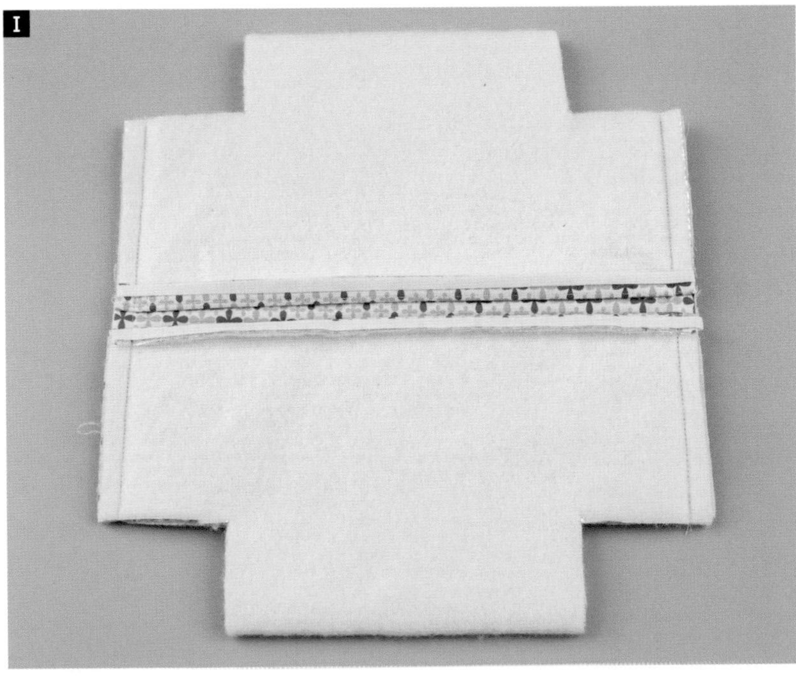

6 Sew the corners of the lining following steps 1 and 2 of the Make the Corners section on page 91.

ATTACH THE LINING

1 Open the exterior and insert the lining so the wrong sides are together. Line up the corners and edges as well as you can so that the lining fits inside the exterior piece and all the seams are aligned. Remove the paper strips from the double-sided adhesive tape. Use your fingers to press the tape strips on the lining to the wrong side of the zipper. Make sure things are lined up nicely (J).

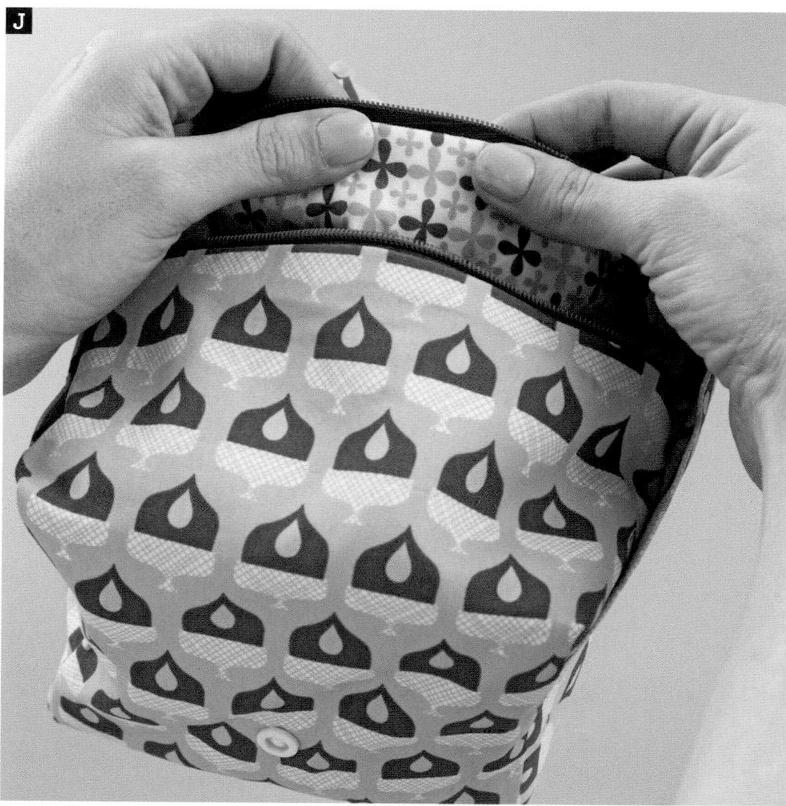
J

2 Topstitch the lining in place around the zipper from the exterior side so that the stitches appear nice and straight from the outside (see Topstitching, page xii). Use a zipper foot if needed. The lining may also be sewn to the zipper by hand if you do not wish stitching to show on the outside of the tote (K).

K

3 Snap the handle in place!

123456
#lovetosew

Patchwork Calculator Tablet Case

Designed by Heidi Staples

LEVEL

Hide a small tablet in this old-school, calculator-style zipper case! The side zip makes it easy to hold a device up to 7½" tall × 6" wide/19cm × 15cm. Copy and transfer the image for the number screen, or use your own "texty" fabric instead.

***Note:** If you place the zipper at the top, instead of the side, it will accommodate a slightly taller tablet, with dimensions up to 8" x 5½"/20.5cm × 14cm.*

FINISHED SIZE Approximately 7¼" × 9¼"/18.5cm × 23.5cm
SEAM ALLOWANCE Use ¼"/6mm seam allowance, unless otherwise noted

What You Need

FABRIC

Suggested fabrics include light- to medium-weight cotton and cotton blends.

- ¼yd/23cm (or 1 fat quarter) of solid color fabric for the exterior
- ¼yd/23cm (or 1 fat quarter) of lining fabric
- ¼yd/23cm (or 1 fat quarter) of muslin
- 16 scraps of various colored prints, at least 1½"/4cm square for the calculator buttons
- Scrap of white (or number print) fabric, 2" × 6"/5cm × 15cm, for the calculator screen
- Template, page 120

TIP I like to cut the entire 2" × 6"/5cm × 15cm design out of TAP instead of trimming around the numbers. This makes the surface of the entire rectangle feel a bit "screenlike" and more interesting. Be sure to cut inside the lines, or you might accidentally transfer them to your ironing board.

ADDITIONAL SUPPLIES

- ¼yd/23cm of quilt batting
- Transfer Artist Paper (TAP) for printing a calculator screen (optional)
- Fine-tip marker (optional)
- Basting spray
- Zipper foot
- 1 zipper, at least 10"/25.5cm long
- Chopstick or turning tool

What You Do

CUT YOUR FABRIC

From the exterior fabric, cut:

- 12 strips, 1" × 1½"/2.5 × 4cm, for between the buttons
- 4 strips, 1" × 6"/2.5cm × 15cm, for between the screen and buttons
- 4 strips, 1½" × 8"/4cm × 20.5cm, for the frame around the calculator buttons and screen
- 1 back, 7¾" × 9¾"/19.5cm × 25cm

From the interior fabric, cut:

- 2 lining pieces, 7¾" × 9¾"/19.5cm × 25cm

From the batting, cut:

- 2 pieces, 7¾" × 9¾"/19.5cm × 25cm

From the muslin, cut:

- 2 pieces, 7¾" × 9¾"/19.5cm × 25cm

From the colored print scraps, cut:

- 16 squares, 1½" × 1½"/4cm × 4cm

From the white or the number-print fabric, cut:

- 1 calculator screen, 2" × 6"/5cm × 15cm

CREATE THE CALCULATOR SCREEN WITH TRANSFER ARTIST PAPER (TAP)

This step is optional if you would rather use a number-print fabric.

1 Use a flatbed inkjet (not laser) color printer to photocopy the calculator screen design (on page 120) onto the white side of the TAP (A).

1a *Alternative method:* Use a fine-tip marker and a lightbox (or hold the pattern up to a window) to trace the calculator screen design onto the white side of Transfer Artist Paper.

2 Cut the calculator screen design from the TAP.

A

3 Place the piece of TAP, with the design side down, on the right side of the white computer screen piece. Press for approximately forty seconds* until the paper peels away easily and the image adheres to the fabric. Refer to the TAP package insert for complete instructions (B).

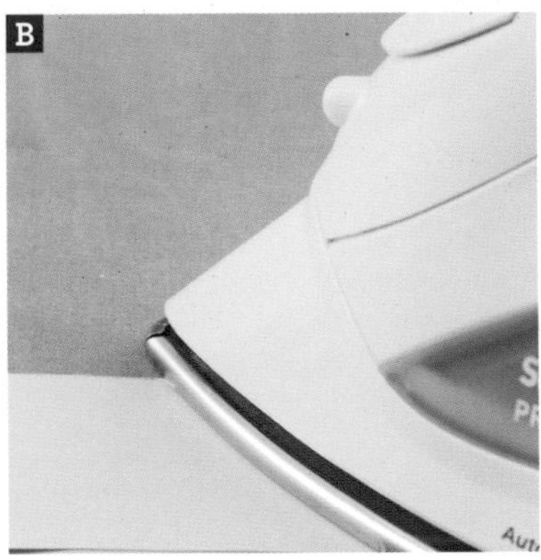

MAKE THE PATCHWORK FRONT

1 Lay out your sixteen calculator buttons in the order in which you want them to appear on the tablet case. Place the 1" × 1½"/2.5cm × 4cm background strips between the buttons. Sew these together into four rows. Press the seams (C).

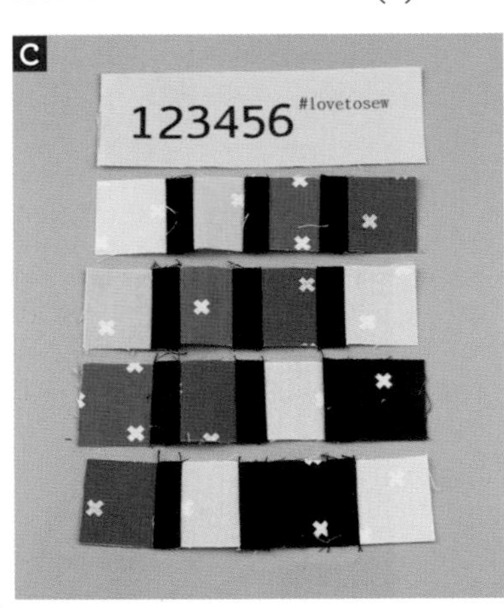

2 Place the 1" x 6"/2.5cm x 15cm background strips between the rows of buttons and the calculator screen. Sew these together into one large rectangle. Press the seams (D).

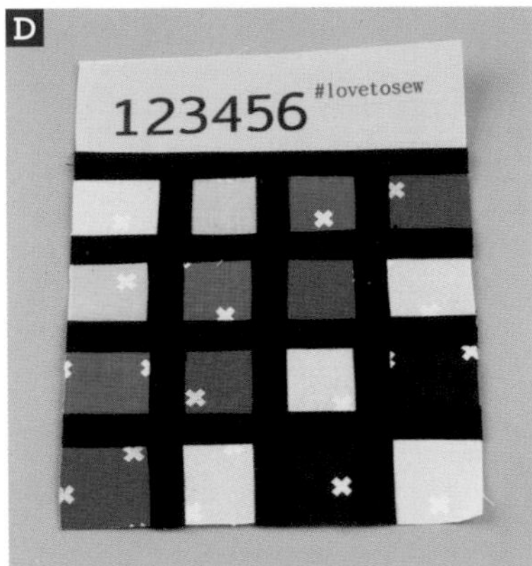

3 Sew two of the 1½" x 8"/4cm x 20.5cm background strips to the right and left of the front rectangle, trimming any excess. Press the seams. Then sew the remaining 1 ½" x 8"/4cm x 20.5cm background strips to the top and bottom of the rectangle. Trim the finished exterior front to 7¾" x 9¾"/19.5cm x 25cm and press (E).

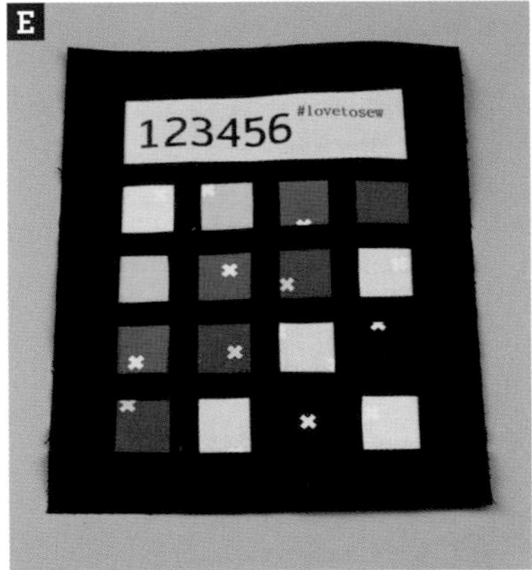

ASSEMBLE THE CASE

1 Use the adhesive basting spray to fuse one piece of muslin to one piece of batting. Then spray-baste the front to the other side of the batting. Machine-quilt as desired. Repeat with the remaining muslin, batting, and exterior back pieces (F).

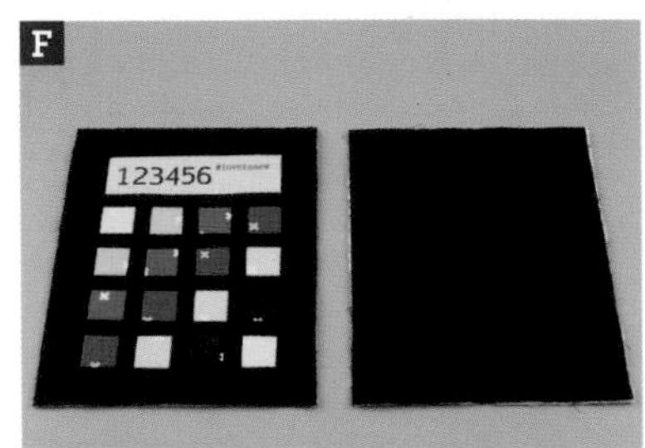

2 Install the zipper foot. Place the zipper, right side down, on the right side of the front of the case, along the right side. Then place one lining piece, right side down over the zipper and the case front. Clip or pin the three layers together and stitch (G).

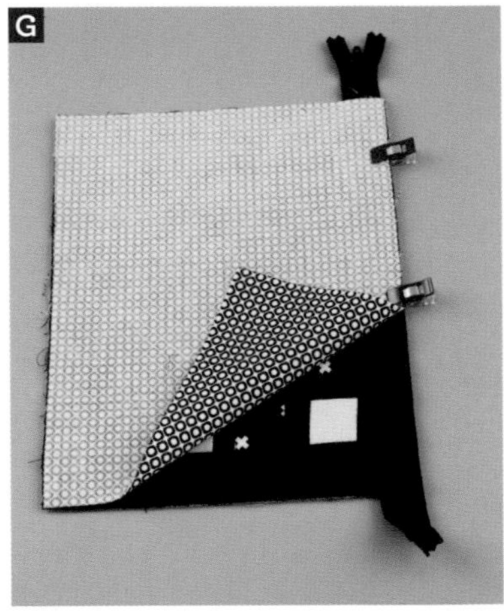

* The TAP instructions state twenty seconds, but I found that the paper peeled away more easily and my image was darker if I held the iron down for twice as much time.

3 Press the exterior and lining pieces away from the zipper so the wrong sides of the fabrics are together. Take care not to melt your zipper. Topstitch ⅛"/3mm from the fold to keep the lining from getting caught in your zipper (see Topstitching, page xii). (H)

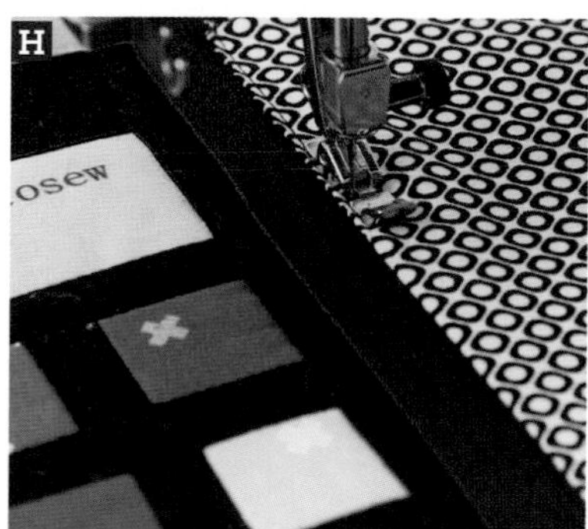

4 Repeat steps 2 and 3 on the opposite side of the zipper with the remaining lining and exterior pieces (I).

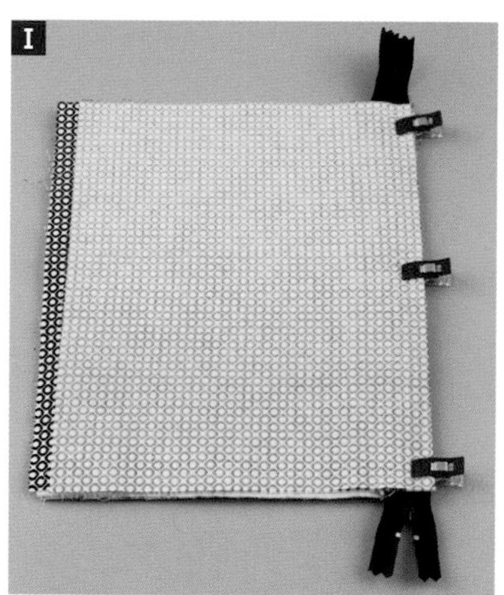

TIP Feel free to quilt the exterior of the case however you would like. I used my sewing machine's walking foot and quilted straight lines on the front piece using the buttons as my guide. On the back, I marked a grid of straight lines, 2"/5cm apart. Then I stitched quilting lines ¼"/6mm on either side of the marked lines. See Straight Line Quilting (page xi).

5 Unzip the zipper at least halfway. Fold the two exterior pieces together with the right sides touching, being sure that the teeth of your zipper point toward the exterior, and pin or clip them together. Do the same with the lining pieces.

6 Sew all the way around the large rectangle (as shown with dotted lines, below), leaving a 6"/15cm opening in the bottom of the lining pieces for turning. Trim the four corners and cut away the ends of the zipper (J).

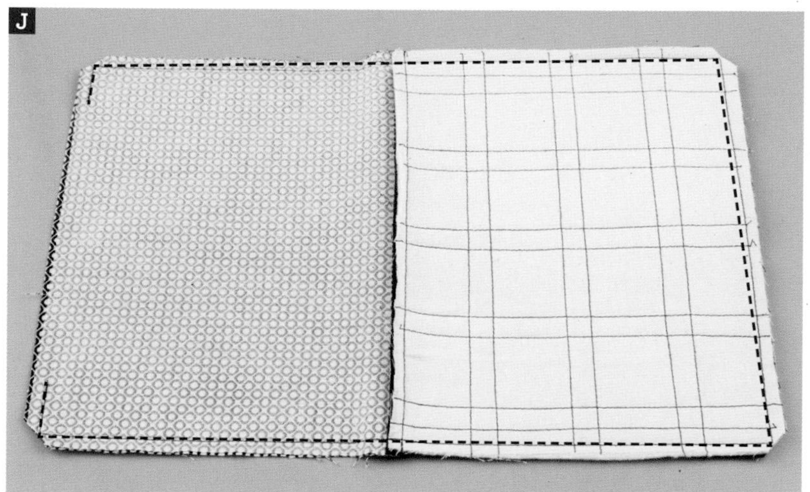

7 Turn the case right side out through the opening in the lining. Use a turning tool to gently push out the corners and press. Sew the opening in the lining closed. Push the lining into the case, zip it closed, and give the case one last pressing to finish.

TEMPLATES AND RESOURCES

Templates

Circle Pouch Shopping Tote, page 3

A

Bag Body Pattern Piece

Cut 2 on Fold from Exterior Fabric
Cut 2 on Fold from Lining Fabric
Enlarge by 400%

Fold

B

Bag Pocket Pattern Piece

Cut 4 from Lining Fabric
Enlarge by 250%

Center Ribbon Piece Here

Divide-and-Conquer Drawstring Bag, page 9

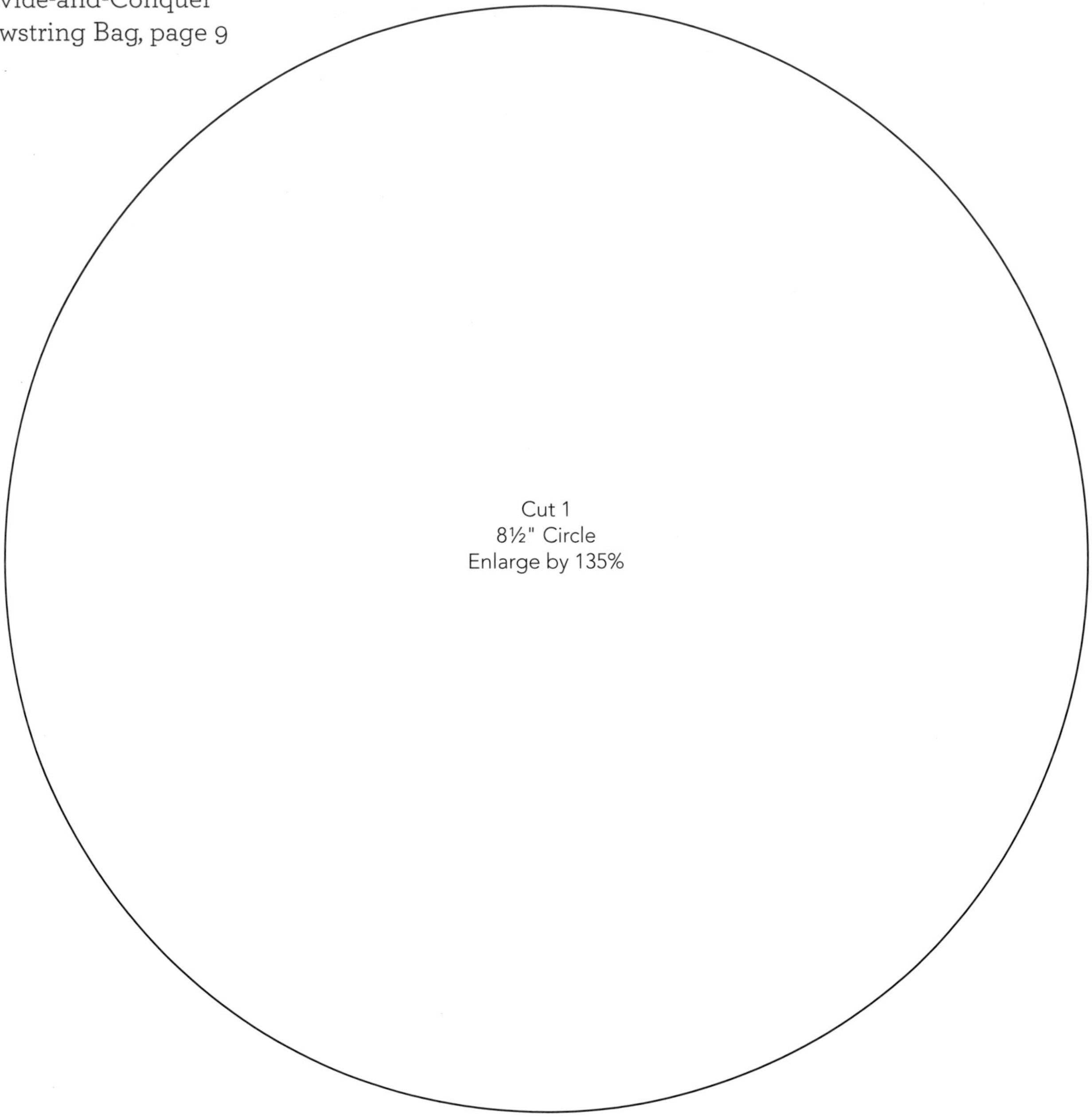

Cut 1
8½" Circle
Enlarge by 135%

(A)

Two-in-One Lunch Tote and Place Mat, page 15

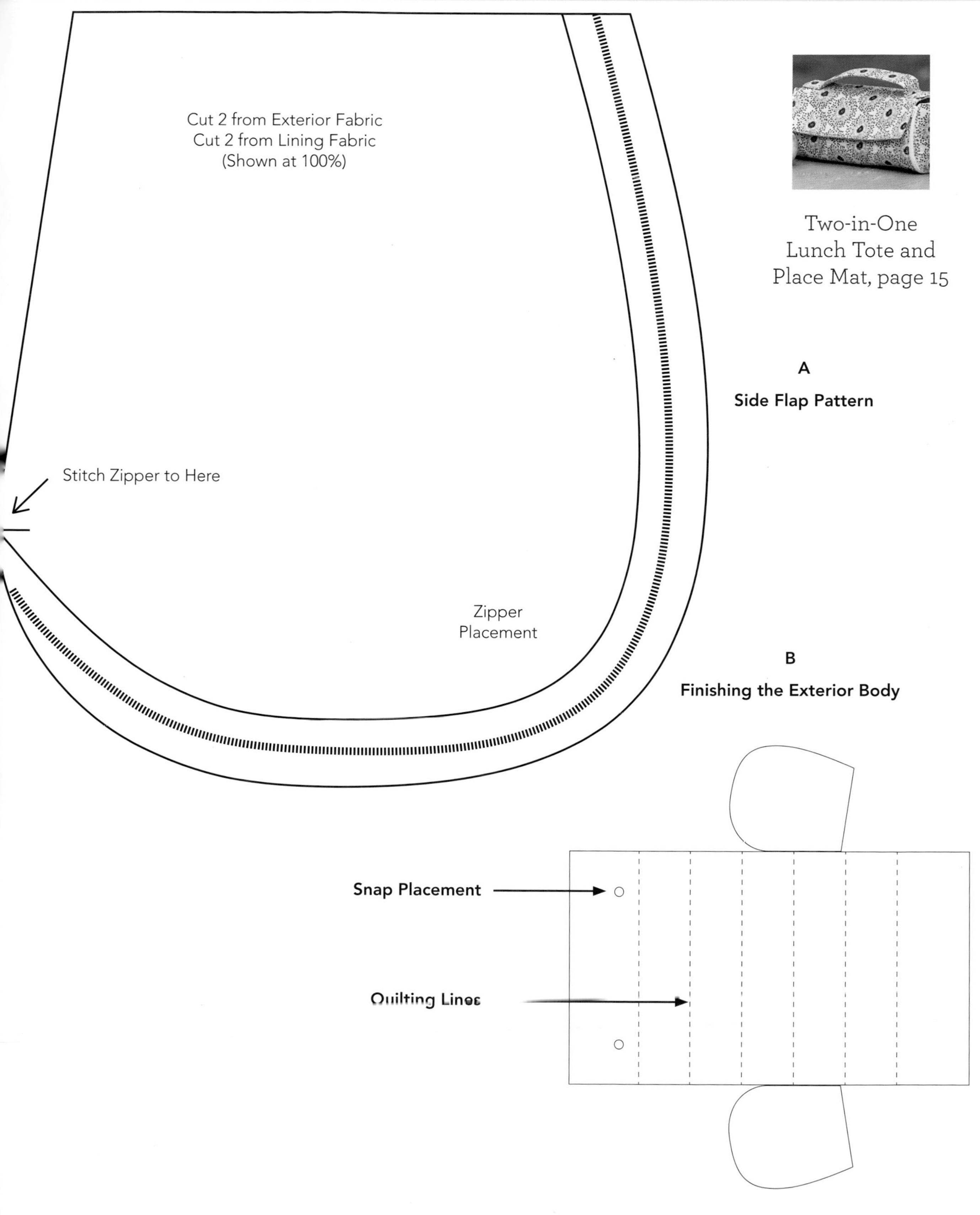

A

Side Flap Pattern

B

Finishing the Exterior Body

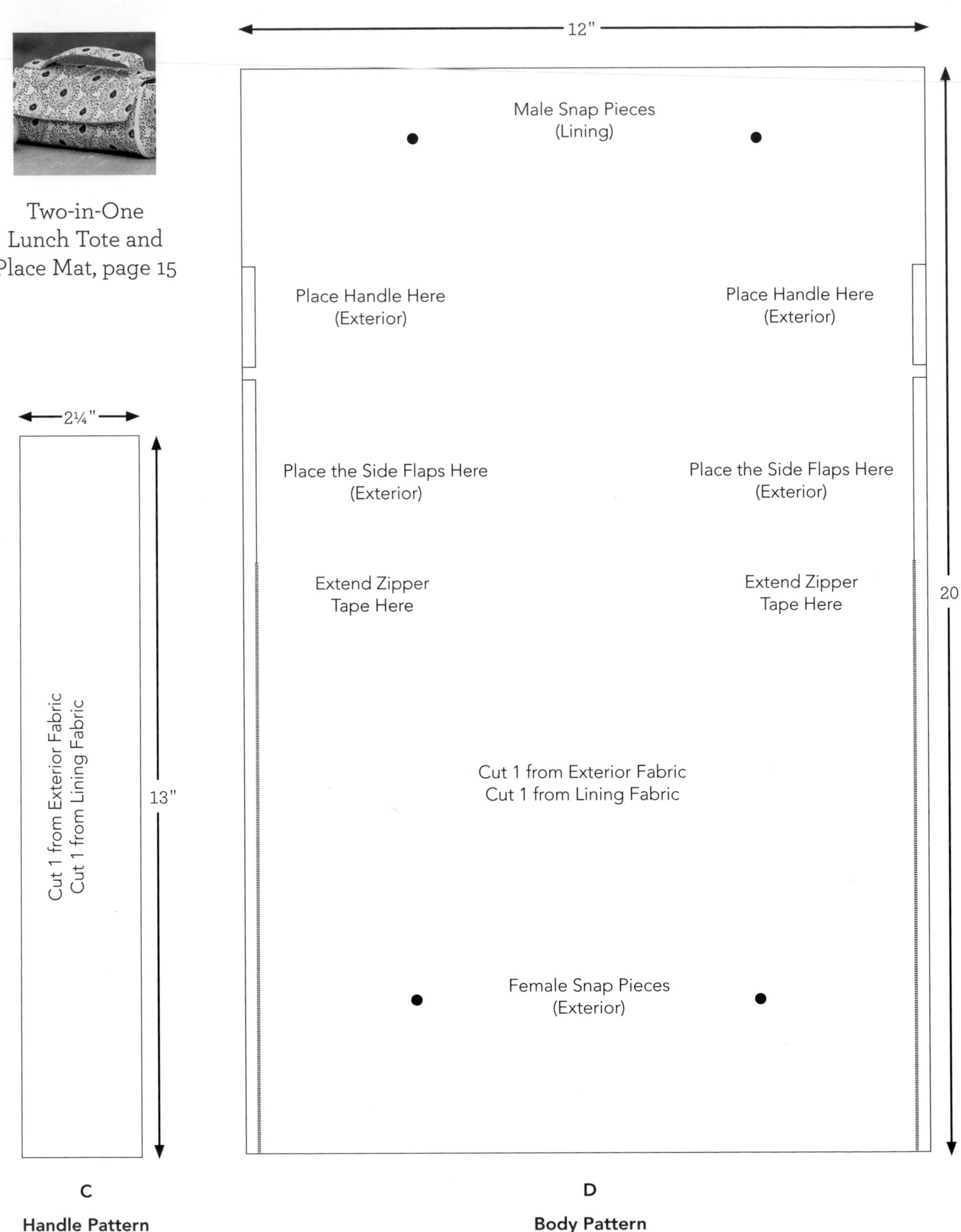

C

Handle Pattern

D

Body Pattern

Quilty First Aid Kit, page 21

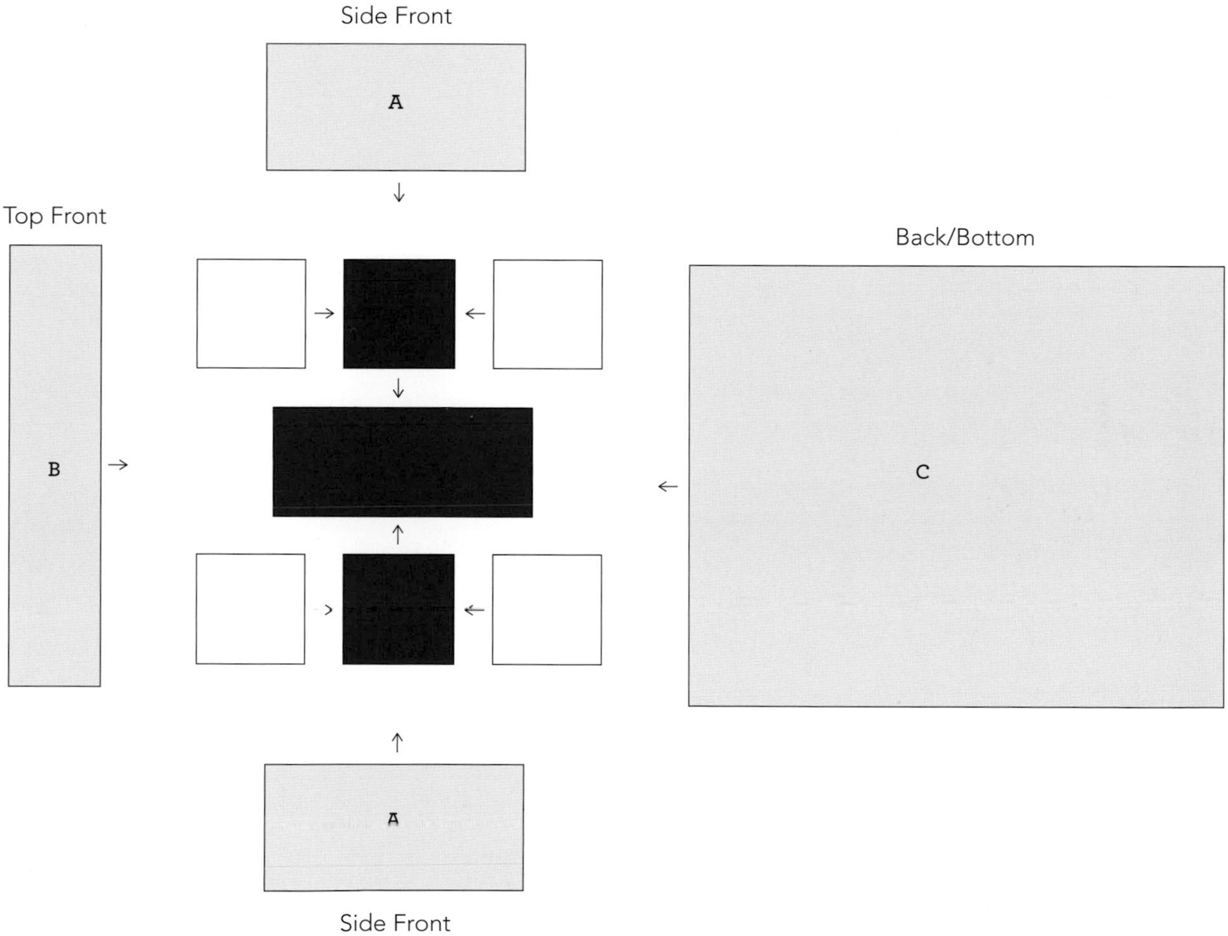

Side Front

A

Top Front

B

Back/Bottom

C

A

Side Front

Assembling the Kit Exterior

Quilty First Aid Kit, page 21

Make Marks 4¼"
from Each Short End

4¼"

Mark the Centers of
the Short End

Marking the Kit Exterior Piece

Casual Couponer Divided Pouch, page 27

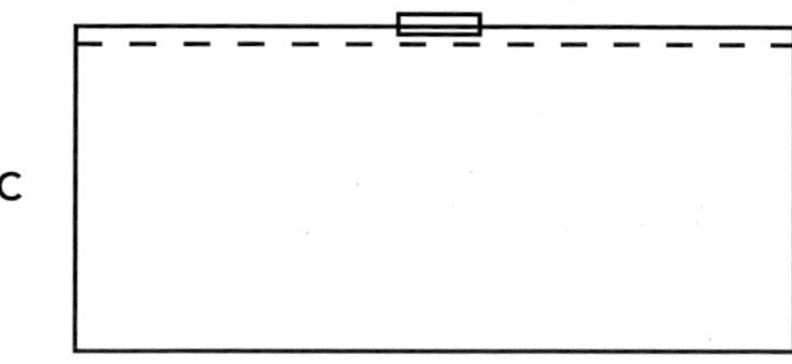

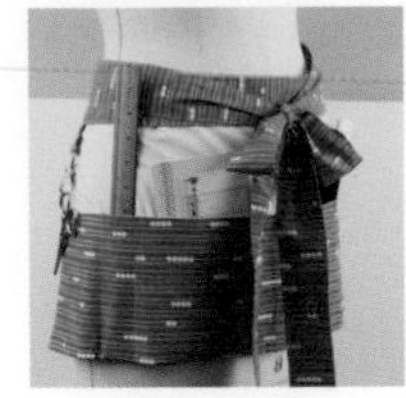

Crafty Biz Apron, page 41

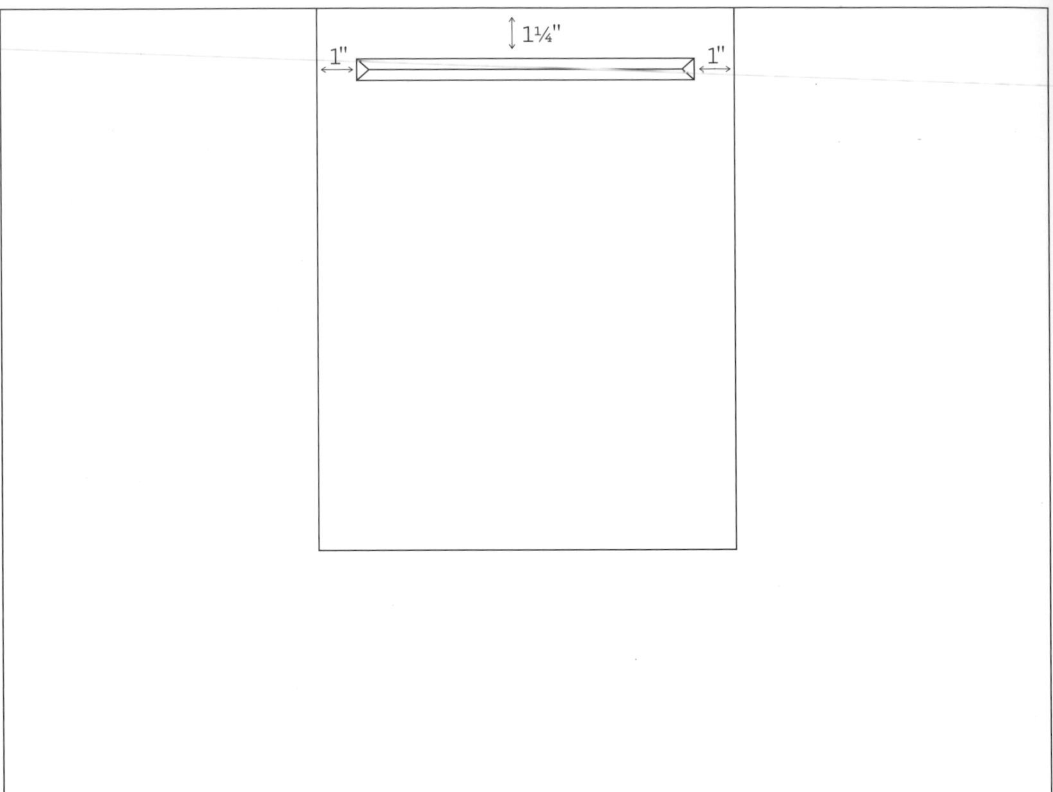

A

Pinning the Hidden Zipper Pocket

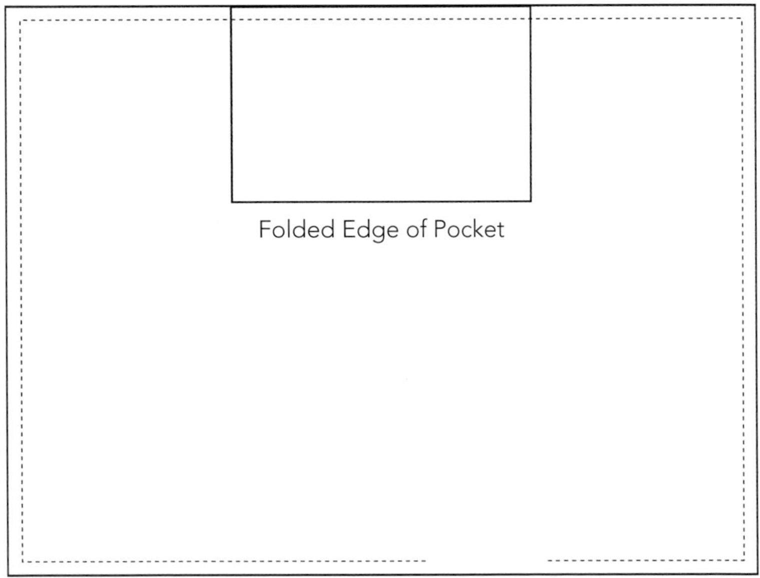

B

Stitching the Apron's Layers Together

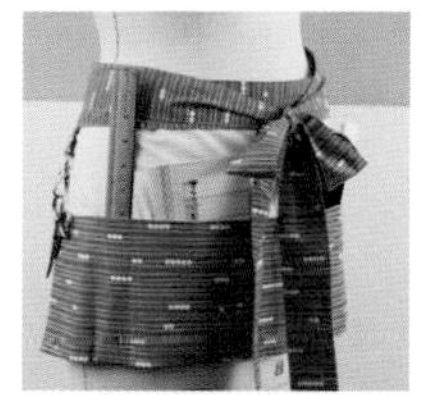

Crafty Biz Apron,
page 41

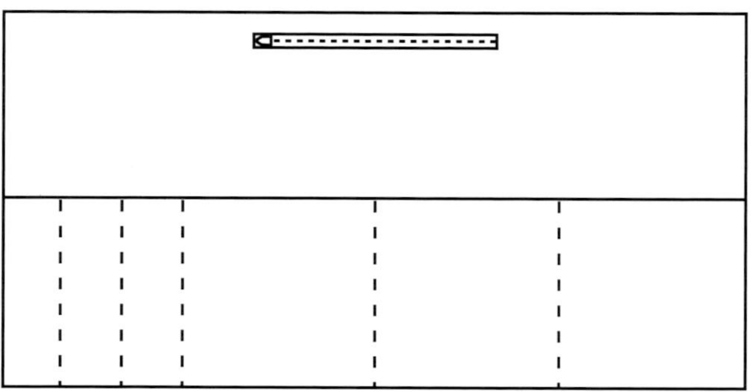

C

Sewing Lines of Pocket Dividers

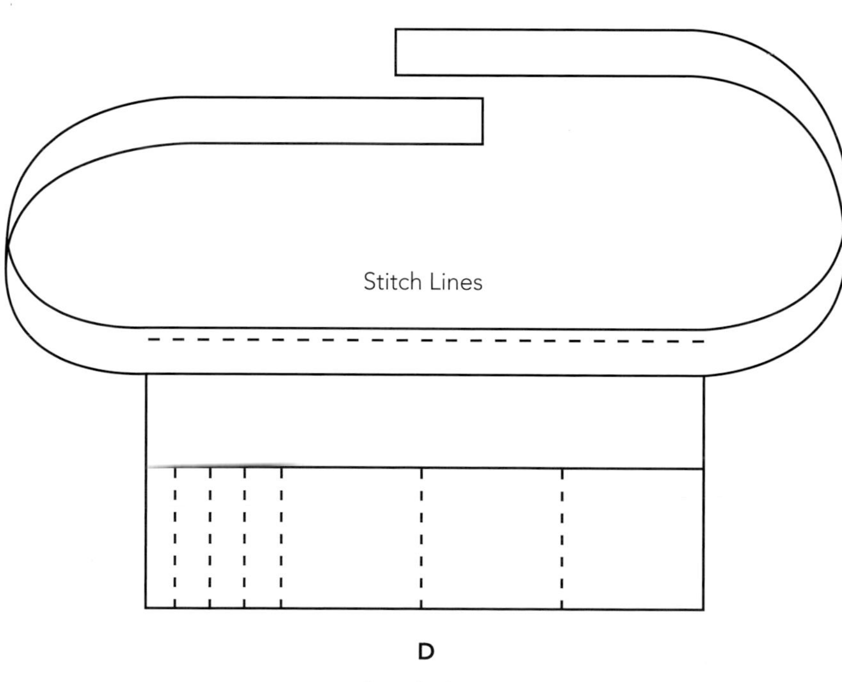

D

Waistband Placement

Reversible Barstool Cushion, page 47

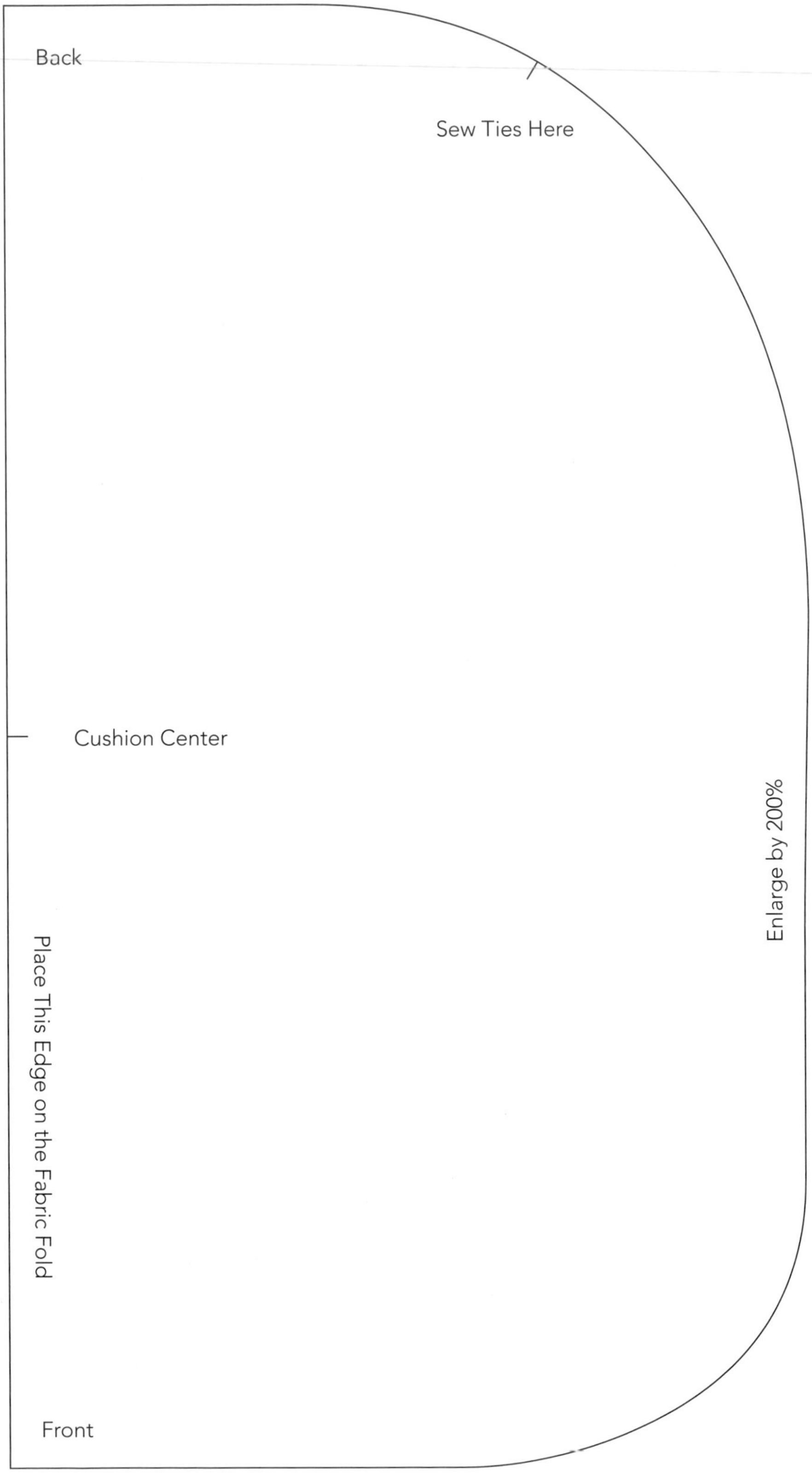

Back

Sew Ties Here

Cushion Center

Place This Edge on the Fabric Fold

Enlarge by 200%

Front

A

Fabric Layout for Apron Body

Everyday Apron,
page 51

Curve Template
Enlarge by 500%

Pocket Template
Enlarge by 500%

B

Fabric Layout for Pockets (and Bias Binding)

Spacious Spa Caddy,
page 55

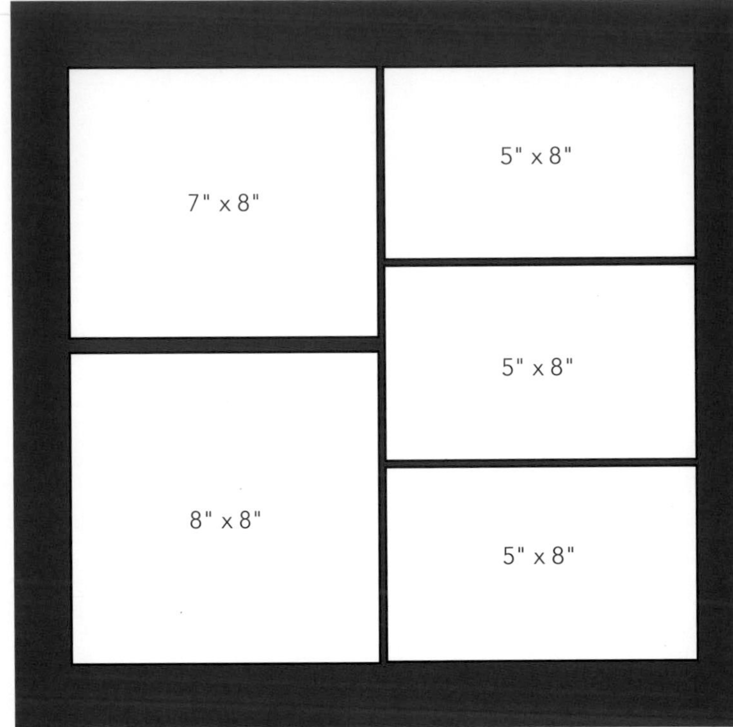

A

Cutting Exterior (If Using Fat Quarters)

5" x 8"
5" x 8"
5" x 8"
5" x 8"
7" x 8"
7" x 8"

Spacious Spa Caddy, page 55

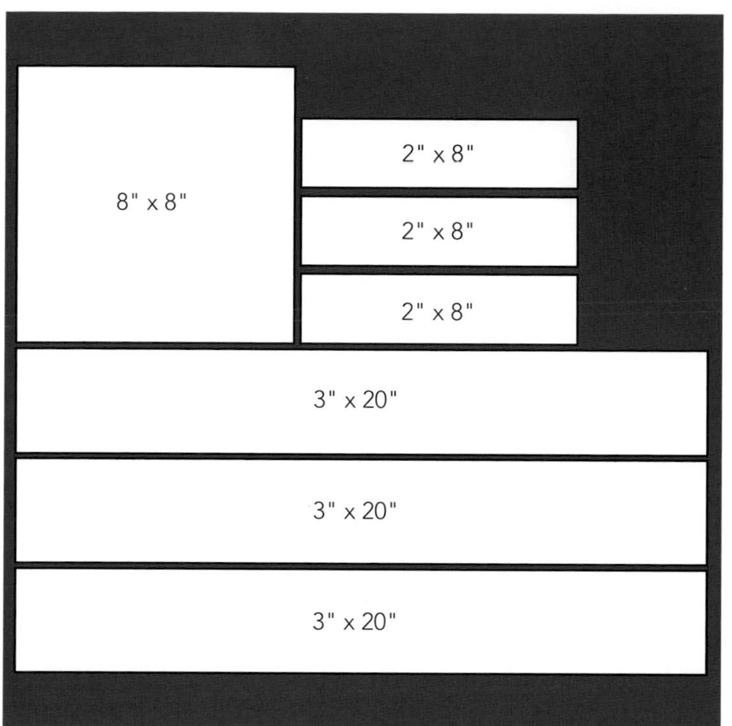

B

Cutting Lining (If Using Fat Quarters)

2" x 13½"—Piece to Make 33" Binding

2" x 20"—Piece to Make 33" Binding

7" x 8"

7" x 8"

7" x 8"

7" x 8"

Spacious Spa Caddy, page 55

C

Marking Lines for Pockets

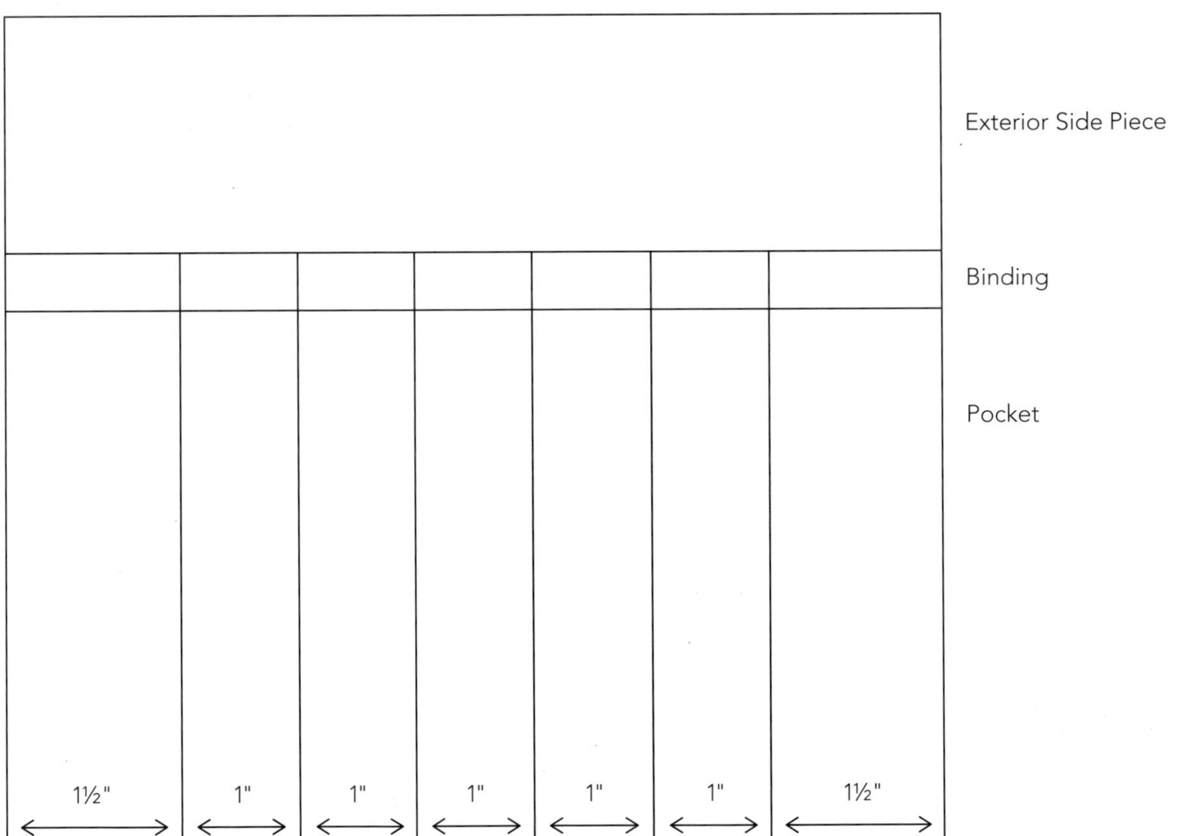

Marking Lines for Pockets

Spacious Spa Caddy, page 55

D

Exterior Basket and Lining

Side Pieces

8 x 8 Bottom Piece

Side Pieces

Photo Frame Fridge Magnet, page 61

A

Template for Magnet

(Shown at 100%)

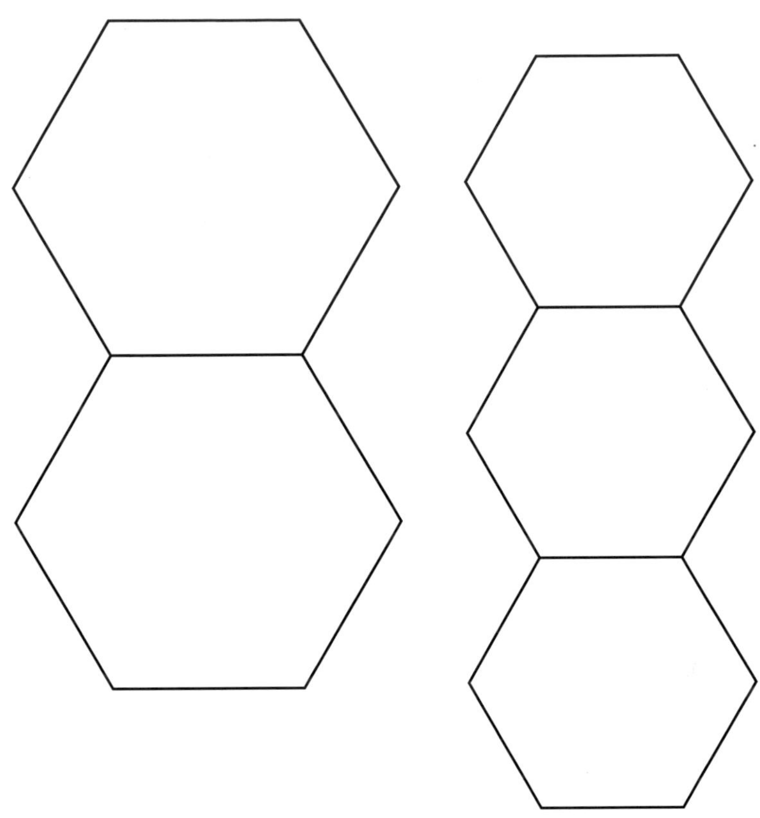

B

Preparing the Frame

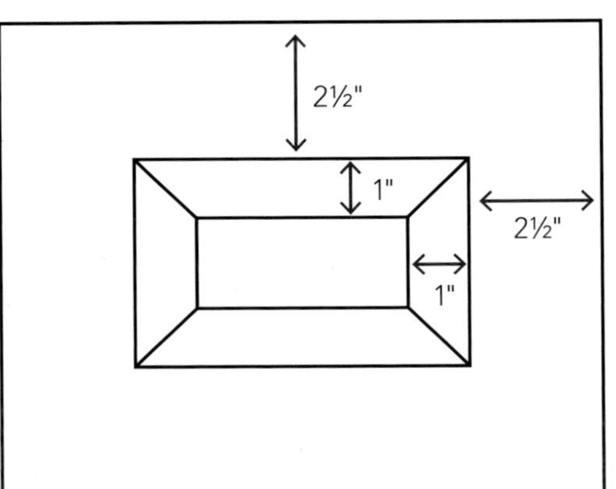

A

Hexi Magnet Template

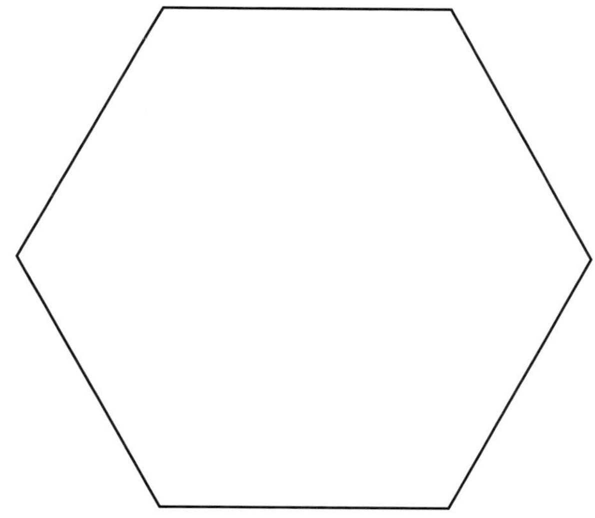

B

Hexi Magnet Template

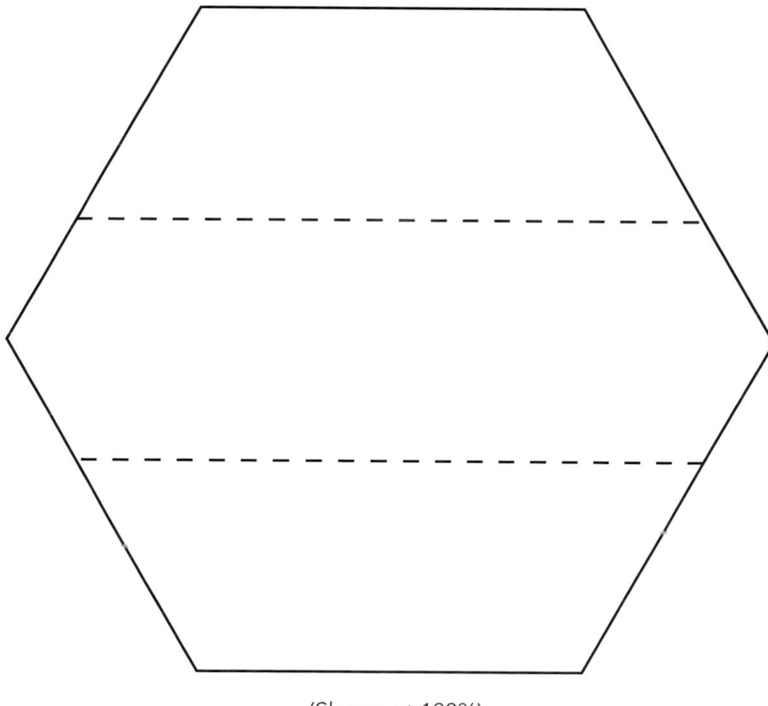

(Shown at 100%)

Cute Hexi Magnets, page 64

Festive
“Buttoned-Up”
Baskets,
page 67

Holly Template

(Shown at 100%)

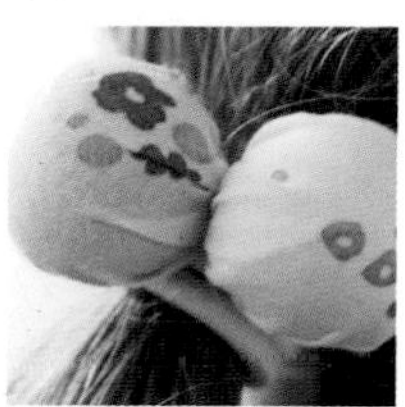

Felt and Fabric Hair Baubles, page 83

3-Inch-Diameter Circle Template

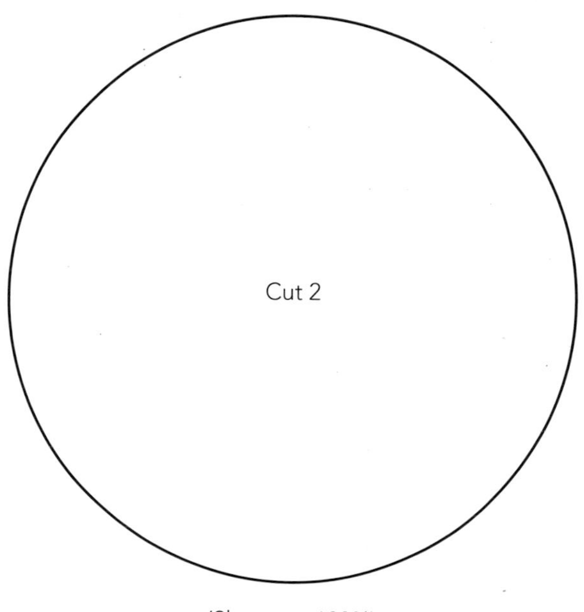

(Shown at 100%)

Color-Block Headband, page 85

A

Fabric Teens'/Women's Headband Pattern

Enlarge by 300%

B

Fabric Girls' Headband Pattern

Enlarge by 300%

C

Elastic Girls' Headband Pattern

Enlarge by 300%

D

Elastic Teens'/Women's Pattern Piece

Enlarge by 300%

Lunch-in-a-Snap Tote,
page 89

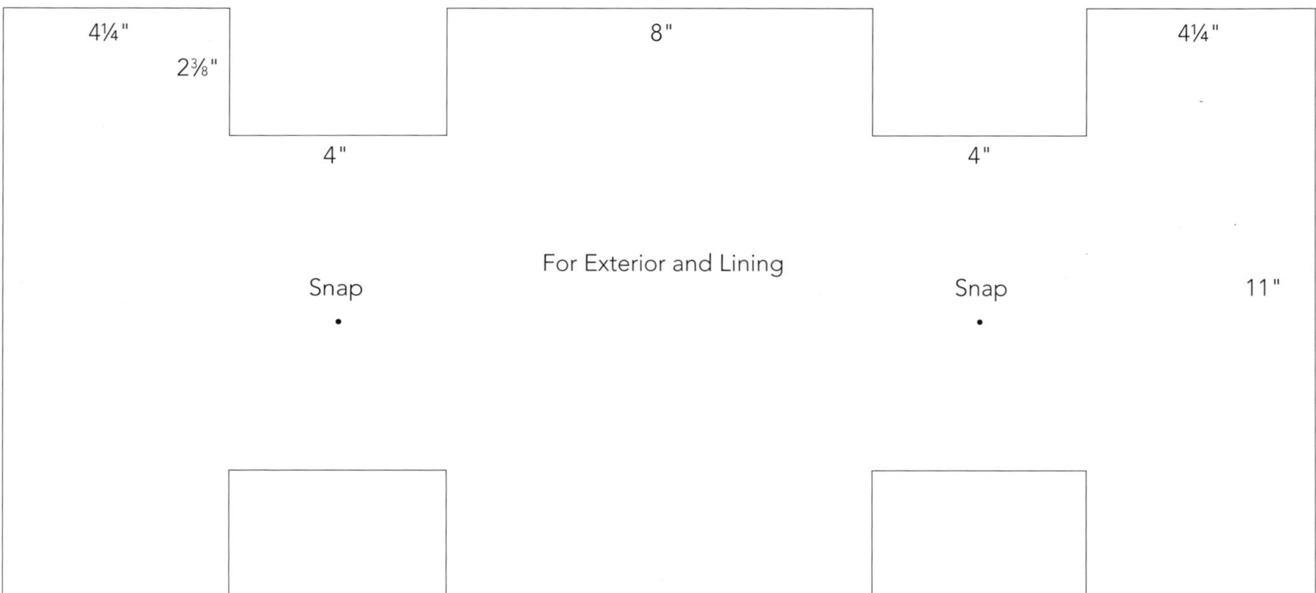

Patchwork Calculator Tablet Case, page 95

123456 #lovetosew

(Shown at 100%)

Fabric and Notions Sources

Casual Couponer Divided Pouch

Fabrics used: Exterior: Little Garden from Monaluna, gray solid; lining: Lighthearted from Kokka

Pellon DecorBond 809 interfacing

Circle Pouch Shopping Tote

Fabrics used: Crossed Impressions and Bullion Fronds from Art Gallery Fabrics

Reversible zipper from www.wawak.com

Fray Check Seam Sealant

Wonder Tape sewing adhesive

Cute Hexi Magnets and Photo Frame Fridge Magnets

Fabrics used: Print fabrics from Cotton + Steel; solids from RJR Fabrics

Peltex 71F from Pellon

Fabric Fuse fabric glue from Thermoweb

Crafty Biz Apron

Fabric used: Abacus Coral and Solid Cream from Birch Fabrics (Fabricworm)

Thermoweb pressing paper

Divide-and-Conquer Drawstring Bag

Fabric used: Wallflower in Poppy from Free Spirit Fabrics

Easy Wallet with Pockets

Fabrics used: Quilting cottons from Cotton + Steel

Pellon 101S woven fusible interfacing

Everyday Apron

Fabric used: Flower Sugar Maison Oxford (home décor-weight cotton) from Lecien

Felt and Fabric Hair Baubles

Fabric used: Lunada Bay Voile from Cloud 9 Fabrics

Festive "Buttoned-Up" Baskets

Fabrics used: All these fabrics are from the "It's Christmas" collection by Jennifer Heynen for In The Beginning Fabrics.

Peltex 70 from Pellon

Kiddie Backpack

Fabrics used: The Adventurers by Cori Dantini for Blend Fabrics

HeatnBond fusible fleece

Lunch-in-a-Snap Tote

Fabrics used: Acorn and Jacks from Monaluna Fabrics

Pellon 101S woven fusible interfacing

Insul-Fleece insulated batting

Wonder Tape sewing adhesive

Patchwork Calculator Tablet Case

Fabrics used: Cotton Couture Solids from Michael Miller Fabrics; XOXO Basics from Cotton and Steel Fabrics

Lesley Riley's TAP Transfer Artist Paper

SpraynBond basting spray

Quilty First Aid Kit

Fabrics used: Scraps of fabric from Caroline's stash; Warm and White cotton batting

SpraynBond basting spray

Reversible Barstool Cushion

Fabrics used: Flower Sugar Maison Oxford (home décor-weight cotton) from Lecien

Soft n Crafty Hi-Loft Batting by Fairfield

HeatnBond medium-weight fusible interfacing

HeatnBond fusible fleece

Snappy Supply Case

Fabrics used: Briar rose by Heather Ross for Windham Fabrics

Warm and White cotton batting

Wonder Tape sewing adhesive

Spacious Spa Caddy

Fabric used: Ribbon Bloom and Painted Woodgrain by Josephine Kimberling for Blend Fabrics

Pellon 101S woven fusible interfacing

Peltex 70 extra-firm fusible interfacing from Pellon

Take-Along Ironing Mats

Fabrics for larger mat: Wordplay by Michele D'Amore for Benartex; ironing board utility fabric.

Fabrics for FQ-friendly mat: Vintage Floral by Melody Miller for Cotton + Steel Fabrics; Moonlit by Rashida Coleman-Hale for Cotton + Steel Fabrics.

Insul-Bright insulated batting

Fray Check Seam Sealant

Two-In-One Lunch Tote and Place Mat

Fabrics used: Clover Field and Thru the Wire from Art Gallery Fabrics

By Annie's Flexible Foam Stabilizer

About the Author and Project Designers

Caroline Fairbanks-Critchfield (author) hand-picked twelve of the crafty sewing projects in this book from ideas suggested by her favorite bloggers and designed the rest (Circle Pouch Shopping Tote, page 3; Two-in-One Lunch Tote and Place Mat, page 15; Take-Along Ironing Mats, page 31; Crafty Biz Apron, page 41; Reversible Barstool Cushion, page 47; Everyday Apron, page 51; Kiddie Backpack, page 73; and Easy Wallet with Pockets, page 79). She is the enthusiastic sewist and author behind the popular blog SewCanShe. See her on *It's Sew Easy* TV (series 1200) or in her Craftsy class, Colorful Patchwork Bags and Baskets. She also co-authored *Just For You: Selfish Sewing Projects From Your Favorite SewCanShe Bloggers* (Stash Books, 2014). In her free time she raises four kids and keeps a semi-organized home. Once upon a time (it seems) she studied Russian language and literature at Brigham Young University. Now she shares sewing expertise and ideas with anyone who wants to learn.

website: **SewCanShe.com**

Jenelle Clark (Photo Frame Fridge Magnet, page 61, Cute Hexi Magnets, page 64) is a self-taught quilter and sewist with a particular passion for hand-sewing. She comes from a background in landscape architecture and studio art, which continues to influence her design process and shape the way she approaches making modern quilts. Never too far from a needle and thread, she especially loves English paper piecing, stashing beautiful fabrics, and working with bold colors. She keeps a journal of her creative pursuits at her blog, Echinops & Aster. Jenelle currently lives with her husband and kitty in Seattle, where she works in nonprofits and revels daily in the natural beauty of the Pacific Northwest.

website: **echinopsaster.blogspot.com**

Jennifer Heynen (Festive "Buttoned-Up" Baskets, page 67) has been a self-supporting artist for nineteen years, first making ceramic beads and jewelry and now designing, sewing, and crafting projects. She is currently designing her fourteenth line of fabric for In The Beginning Fabrics. Jennifer has a line of sewing patterns and kits she designs under the name "Jennifer Jangles." If she's not driving her boys to and from activities, she can be found in her Athens, Georgia, studio making Happy Things.

website: **jenniferjangles.com**

Becky Jorgensen (Snappy Supply Case, page 33) is the designer and owner of Patchwork Posse. She started her sewing journey at age eight—with a stitched sampler to show for it. Sewing has always been part of her life, but when her first child was born, it blossomed into her career. Starting with her first baby quilt, then a quilt-block sampler, she found that designing patterns and quilts for others was what she wanted to pursue. Her designs have been published in *Primitive Quilts and Projects* magazine, *Craft Ideas*, and *Fat Quarterly*. In addition, she has designed for Andover Fabrics, Thermoweb, the Ribbon Retreat, Moda Bake Shop, and others. Exploring new techniques, ideas and mediums, she is always trying something new—pushing the boundaries in quilts, plushies, dolls, and more.

website: **PatchworkPosse.com**

An Kuppens (Felt and Fabric Hair Baubles, page 83; Color-Block Headband, page 85) is a pattern designer and sewing blogger who lives in Belgium. She started sewing shortly after the birth of her eldest daughter and then began studying pattern design. Upon the success of her first patterns for children's clothing, An left her job in academia in 2015 to become a full-time pattern designer. An has a soft spot for clean and minimalist designs with a special detail or original touch. Besides children's wear, her patterns and tutorials also include home decoration and baby essentials. She lives in Antwerp with her husband and daughters, Norah and Ava.

website: **straight-grain.com**

Pattern designer and sewist **Virginia Lindsay** (Lunch-in-a-Snap Tote, page 89) is the creator of Gingercake Patterns and the author of the blog Gingercake. She is the author of two books: *Sewing to Sell: The Beginner's Guide to Starting a Craft Business* (Stash Books, 2014), and *Pretty Birds: 18 projects to Sew and Love* (Running Press, 2015). Virginia also has had several of her patterns published by Simplicity. She loves to create fun, unique, and useful projects that make sewing time an enjoyable and treasured experience. Her most popular sewing patterns include whimsical pillows, notebook covers, lunch bags, and crayon holders. Virginia lives in Freeport, Pennsylvania, with her husband, Travis, and four children who inspire her every day. She also loves to garden, decorate, and take walks with her overly zealous Labrador Retriever, Woody.

website: **www.gingercake.org**

Sarah Markos (Casual Couponer Divided Pouch, page 27) is a stay-at-home mom who loves all things fabric-related. She started sewing at an early age, but really learned to love it as a teenager when she took apart her favorite pair of pants and used it as a pattern to make a new pair. She started designing and sewing handbags to sell at local holiday fairs as a way to use up her ever-growing fabric stash. Sarah lives in West Melbourne, Florida, with her husband and five children. She has a BS in nursing from Brigham Young University and enjoys telling her kids gory stories from her life as an operating room nurse. She also loves running, reading to her children, and teaching people how to sew. She blogs about her sewing adventures at Blue Susan Makes.

website: **bluesusanmakes.blogspot.com**

Christina Roy (Spacious Spa Caddy, page 55) resides in New Hampshire with her husband and is a stay-at-home mother to their three children. For as long as Christina can remember, she has had a passion for creating things. It wasn't until after the birth of their first child, however, that her passion for sewing really evolved and it hasn't stopped growing since. She enjoys sewing just about anything, but loves nothing more than seeing her own kids dressed in her creations. Because her youngest will enter school this fall, she will look forward to utilizing her newfound free time by selling her designs. When Christina is not at her sewing machine, you can find her gardening, working on home renovations, or doing some other DIY project with the kids.

website: **2littlehooligans.com**

Heidi Staples (Patchwork Calculator Tablet Case, page 95) spent ten years in education before becoming a full-time mom in 2009. A few years spent chasing her three little girls around the house convinced her that she needed a hobby and, in the fall of 2011, she sewed her first quilt. That quickly led to a full-blown fabric addiction, an ongoing parade of handmade projects, and the writing of her first book, *Sew Organized for the Busy Girl* (Stash Books, 2015). Heidi lives with her fun-loving family in Texas, and you can follow her sewing misadventures on her blog, Fabric Mutt.

website: **fabricmutt.blogspot.com**

Tessa Walker (Quilty First Aid Kit, page 21) was born in the UK and moved to the United States as a child. She now resides in sunny Florida with her husband, children, two dogs, and a hedgehog. Her grandmother was an accomplished seamstress and Tessa thinks she inherited her grandmother's genes, as she has always loved to sew and began collecting fabric while working in a fabric store in high school. After having made everything from clothes, drapes, and pillows to fine heirloom baby gowns and embroidery, she turned her attention to quilting several years ago and has been obsessed ever since. To chronicle her quilting journey, she started a blog, the Sewing Chick, and has been delighted with the positive response and warm sewing community. It has become her passion to blend traditional quilt patterns with today's colorful, contemporary fabrics, while achieving fine craftsmanship, and she enjoys inspiring others to explore their creativity and get sewing!

website: **thesewingchick.blogspot.com**

Beth Wood (Divide-and-Conquer Drawstring Bag, page 9) is a graphic designer/art director living in Los Angeles. She got her start crafting as a child, growing up in the wilds of Oregon. She learned to sew and knit in grade school and has been making her own clothes ever since. Today she authors the website Sew DIY, featuring inspiration, tutorials, and sewing patterns for creating your own DIY wardrobe.

website: **SewDIY.com**

Index

Pages in italic refer to project templates

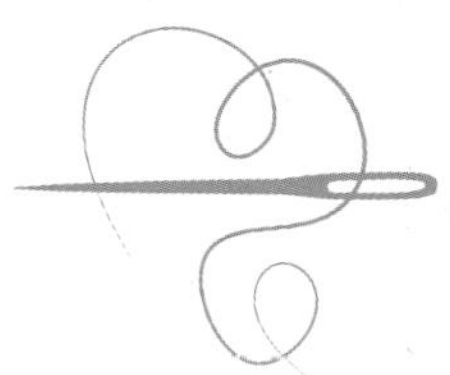